# Carnegie's Dinosaurs

All photographs not otherwise acknowledged by
Vincent J. Abromitis
Catalog Design and Illustrations by Dolores Kacsuta
Parks
Printing by Geyer Printing Company, Inc., Pittsburgh,
Pennsylvania
Typeset in English Times Roman

Library of Congress Card Number: 82-70212
ISBN 0-911239-00-6
Manufactured in the United States of America
©1982 The Board of Trustees, Carnegie Institute,
Pittsburgh, Pennsylvania
Second printing, 1986

# Carnegie's Dinosaurs

**A Comprehensive Guide to Dinosaur Hall
at Carnegie Museum of Natural History,
Carnegie Institute**

by Helen J. McGinnis
Edited by Martina M. Jacobs and Ruth Anne Matinko

The Board of Trustees, Carnegie Institute, Pittsburgh, Pennsylvania

**Key**

**Triassic**
1. marine and fresh-water Triassic fossils
2. *Metoposaurus* skulls

**Jurassic**
3. marine Jurassic fossils
• 4. *Allosaurus*
• 5. *Stegosaurus*
• 6. *Diplodocus*
7. *Diplodocus* thigh bone
• 8. *Apatosaurus*
• 9. *Camptosaurus*
• 10. *Dryosaurus*
11. *Camarasaurus* skull
12. *Diplodocus* skull
13. *Diplodocus* skull and neck vertebrae
• 14. young *Camarasaurus*
15. Jurassic pterosaurs

**Cretaceous**
16. Marine Cretaceous fossils
17. *Polyglyphanodon*
18. Cretaceous foliage
• 19. *Protoceratops*
20. *Tyrannosaurus rex* skull
21. *Tyrannosaurus rex* teeth
22. *Triceratops* skull
• 23. *Tyrannosaurus rex*
24. mural of *Tyrannosaurus rex*
• 25. *Corythosaurus*
26. Cretaceous pterosaurs
27. mural of Kansas' Niobrara Sea

• = *Carnegie's complete dinosaur skeletons*

◀ Cenozoic Hall

# Dinosaur Hall

◀ Paleozoic Hall

# Contents

# Foreword

Collecting, preserving, studying and exhibiting dinosaurs and related fauna have long been an integral and significant part of the history of Carnegie Museum of Natural History, Carnegie Institute. From the heyday of collecting during the first decades of this century to current fieldwork, the accumulation of dinosaur fossils has paralleled the growth of the Museum itself as both a center for scientific research and public programs. To the general public, this association has led many to call our Museum "the home of the dinosaurs." To the scholarly world, collection and research activities at Carnegie Museum of Natural History have distinguished it as one of the world's leading institutions in the search for scientific understanding of these fascinating reptiles.

Given this historical and continuing tradition, the publication of this popular guide to the Museum's Dinosaur Hall is long overdue. *Carnegie's Dinosaurs* is the product of a fine collaborative effort involving individuals from our scientific, education and exhibit sections. The book's primary author, Helen J. McGinnis, first joined the Museum's Section of Vertebrate Fossils in 1970 as a Research Assistant. She worked with the Section through 1974, leaving then to pursue additional graduate work in the field of Wildlife Management. Despite her new career, Helen's attachment to the Museum and particularly the dinosaur collection did not wane. She worked periodically on special projects for the Section, one of which was the ambitious task of researching and writing the original manuscript for this volume.

Dr. Mary R. Dawson, Chief Curator of Earth Sciences and Curator of Vertebrate Fossils, served as the primary scientific advisor to the project, reviewing the refinement of the manuscript through its various phases. The creation of a popular guide to the dinosaur collection has long been dear to Mary's heart. Her perserverance and dedication to this effort have at last been rewarded by this publication.

Dr. Leonard Krishtalka, Associate Curator of Vertebrate Fossils, also provided extensive advice and editorial assistance throughout the project. In addition, valuable contributions to the text were made by Associate Curators Dr. John E. Guilday

and Dr. David S. Berman of the Section of Vertebrate Fossils, as well as by the Curator of Invertebrate Fossils, Dr. John L. Carter.

The tasks of final editing and coordination of production were superbly carried out by Dr. Martina M. Jacobs, Program Specialist for Publications, and Ruth Anne Matinko, Program Assistant for Publications, in the Section of Education. Emmy Magel, Head Docent, and members of the Museum's docent staff enthusiastically spent hours in the refinement of the manuscript. Carol March of the Section of Exhibits ably performed the job of typesetting the text. The handsome visual presentation of *Carnegie's Dinosaurs* is the fine work of graphic designer Dolores Kacsuta Parks. We also commend the work of Geyer Printing Company, Inc.

A special acknowledgement must go to photographer Vincent J. Abromitis and audio-visual technician William May who undertook a most challenging assignment. Through ingenious techniques and many hours of painstaking work, Vince and Bill have produced an extraordinary photographic documentation of Dinosaur Hall. The high quality of the photographs in the guide attest to their fine effort. We also thank Timothy Parks, Assistant Director for Public Programs, who coordinated the efforts of the many individuals in the various sections in making this guide a reality.

Finally, we acknowledge The Claude Worthington Benedum Foundation which, through the Benedum Endowment for Public Programs at Carnegie Museum of Natural History, Carnegie Institute, provided financial support for the total project. While dinosaurs became extinct millions of years ago, interest in them, both scientific and popular, is timeless. We present this guide to all visitors to Dinosaur Hall providing more information to those already afflicted by the condition Mary Dawson calls "dinosaurophilia" and whetting the appetites of those still in the early stages of that condition.

Craig C. Black, Director
Carnegie Museum of Natural History,
Carnegie Institute

# Introduction

Many, perhaps most, visitors to Carnegie Museum of Natural History are afflicted with an interesting condition that might be labeled "dinosaurophilia." In other words, they like dinosaurs. Few are immune from the condition, which is symptomized by an attraction to these long extinct, varied reptiles. The attraction may be based simply on awe for the strange shapes and fantastic sizes of some of the largest creatures that ever roamed the land; it may be related to collecting and exhibiting these animals in museums; it may be based on scientific curiosity about the approximately 125 million years when dinosaurs were the dominant land dwellers, about how dinosaurs moved, ate, slept, lived, and died; it may center on some of the still unsolved puzzles of dinosaurs—were they warm- or cold-blooded, how and where did they rear their young, and why did no dinosaurs survive past the end of the Mesozoic, around 65 million years ago. Dinosaurophilia does not respect age, philosophy, profession. Young and old, scientist and romantic, teacher and pupil—all succumb to it.

Even Pittsburgh's great industrialist and philanthropist Andrew Carnegie was not immune from the attraction of dinosaurs. In 1898, shortly after he had established his museum, Carnegie learned that gigantic beasts were being discovered in the nation's western badlands. Carnegie instructed the Museum's director, W.J. Holland, to "buy this one for Pittsburgh," *this* referring to one of the gigantic sauropod dinosaurs.

Thus began the development of one of the world's outstanding collections of the Mesozoic reptiles grouped under the popular name *dinosaur*. Active, able curators and field collectors, including Jacob Wortman, John Bell Hatcher, and Earl Douglass, went on expeditions that brought back to Pittsburgh numerous bones of dinosaurs from sites in Wyoming, Colorado, Montana, and Utah. The discovery in Wyoming of remarkably complete remains of the sauropod *Diplodocus* led Carnegie to start a program of making replicas that were sent to museums around the world. In 1909 Earl Douglass found a large accumulation of dinosaur bones in northeastern Utah and for years directed excavations at the site that later became Dinosaur National Monument. Now, decades later, Carnegie

Museum paleontologists still explore the world of dinosaurs, solving problems such as what head really belonged to *Apatosaurus,* and excavating sites in the West to add to the research collections and exhibitions of the Museum.

These and other aspects of the involvement of Carnegie Museum of Natural History with dinosaurs are explored in the pages of this book. Each of Carnegie's dinosaurs is featured, famous dinosaur sites are described, and questions of dinosaur ways of life and death are discussed. Other Mesozoic creatures displayed with the dinosaurs in Dinosaur Hall are mentioned as are their roles in the Mesozoic world. In total, *Carnegie's Dinosaurs* will lead you to a closer acquaintance with an outstanding collection of fascinating creatures, the dinosaurs.

Dr. Mary R. Dawson
Chief Curator, Earth Sciences
Curator, Section of Vertebrate Fossils
Carnegie Museum of Natural History,
Carnegie Institute

*Top left: Andrew Carnegie, Pittsburgh industrialist and philanthropist. His interest in dinosaurs provided the impetus for the Museum's vast collection of fossil material. Courtesy of Carnegie Library of Pittsburgh. **Top right:** Young visitors study some of the giants of Dinosaur Hall. **Bottom:** Dinosaur Hall today.*

# The History of the Mesozoic Collection at Carnegie Museum of Natural History

Carnegie Museum's association with dinosaurs and fossils dates back nearly to its founding in 1895. Only three years later, in 1898, Andrew Carnegie became interested in fossils and encouraged his close friend Dr. W.J. Holland to add vertebrate paleontology (the study of fossil animals with backbones) to his expertise. Holland eventually became director of the Museum and, with the personal support of Carnegie, played a major role in assembling what is now one of the finest collections of dinosaurs and other fossils in the world.

When Carnegie became interested in fossils, dinosaurs had already been collected and studied elsewhere in the world. Although a dinosaur now known as *Megalosaurus* was found earlier, the first officially recognized dinosaur remains were discovered in England in 1822. Because of a similarity to modern-day iguanas, English scientists labeled the fossils *Iguanodon*. Not until thirty-some years later were dinosaur bones identified in the United States.

In 1855, fossil teeth were collected from Montana and sent to Dr. Joseph Leidy, a professor of anatomy at the University of Pennsylvania (Philadelphia). Leidy later identified the teeth as belonging to a prehistoric reptile similar to *Iguanodon* which he called *Trachodon*.

In 1858 Leidy was responsible for naming another prehistoric reptile, this one found closer to home in Haddonfield, New Jersey, near Philadelphia. Leidy again recognized a resemblance between these fossil remains and those of *Iguanodon*. He named the reptile *Hadrosaurus* and, from the fossil remains, reconstructed a picture of the animal. With the numerous fossil bones and teeth found for *Hadrosaurus*, Leidy was able to establish solidly the presence of dinosaurs in North America. For his pioneering, Dr. Joseph

Leidy has been subsequently named "the father of American vertebrate paleontology."

During the final thirty years of the nineteenth century, two rival paleontologists, E.D. Cope and O.C. Marsh, described literally tons of dinosaur remains collected throughout Colorado, Wyoming and Montana in the foothills of the Rocky Mountains. The two men were so competitive in their work that each eventually waged a newspaper campaign to discredit the other. Publicity was thus given to their scientific endeavors, and the American populace heard more and more about this scientific study called "vertebrate paleontology."

In 1891, a Department of Vertebrate Paleontology was established at New York's American Museum of Natural History by Henry Fairfield Osborn, one of Cope's early disciples. Dinosaurs were at the top of Osborn's list of priorities, so he dispatched his staff (men who were to become famous in the field of paleontology) to collect, prepare and describe the fossils he intended to acquire. A previously worked quarry at Como Bluff, Wyoming, was reopened, and the excavated dinosaur bones were sent back to the American Museum. Under Osborn's direction, the American Museum soon assumed a prominent role in dinosaur discovery.

Carnegie Museum of Natural History's Department of Vertebrate Paleontology originated some seven years later. The wealth of dinosaurs and other fossils collected by this Department can largely be attributed to the driving force of one man—Andrew Carnegie.

*Left: Throughout the 84 years of his life, Dr. William J. Holland was pastor of Bellefield Presbyterian Church, naturalist for the U.S. Eclipse Expedition to Japan, Chancellor of the University of Pittsburgh, Director of Carnegie Museum of Natural History, and an authority on natural history, world law and entomology. Here Holland holds a page from the revised edition of his publication,* The Butterfly Book. *Courtesy of Carnegie Library of Pittsburgh.*

*Below: Carnegie Museum Vertebrate Fossil Preparation Lab, 1903. In this early photo, staff members are removing dinosaur bones from matrix rock. John Bell Hatcher, then curator of Paleontology and Osteology, is shown seated to the far right.* *Right: William H. Reed, credited with discovering the famous dinosaur quarry at Como Bluff, Wyoming, along with O.C. Marsh. An 1898* New York Journal *headline announcing that Reed had found the "Most Colossal Animal Ever on Earth..." spurred Andrew Carnegie's interest in dinosaurs. Courtesy of American Heritage Center, University of Wyoming.*

*Below: "Most Colossal Animal Ever on Earth Just Found Out West!,"* New York Journal, *November, 1898. Captivated by this article, Andrew Carnegie reportedly jotted a hurried note to Museum Director W.J. Holland. The note, "Dear Chancellor, Buy this for Pittsburgh," along with a $10,000 check set in motion years of exploration and spectacular dinosaur finds by Carnegie Museum.*

# Andrew Carnegie's Gift

Two somewhat different stories have been told about the origins of Andrew Carnegie's burning interest in dinosaurs. One story proposes that Carnegie visited the American Museum around the time that Carnegie Museum was first established. There, Carnegie asked Osborn if it would be possible to duplicate the American Museum's collection for his museum in Pittsburgh. Osborn explained that many of the specimens could probably never be duplicated; he offered, instead, an alternative that Carnegie may have taken as a challenge. Osborn explained that, with well-trained and well-equipped exploring parties, the fossil fields of the West held splendid opportunities for dinosaur collection.

A somewhat more dramatic account of Carnegie's introduction to dinosaurs begins with a bright Sunday morning in November, 1898.[1] Over breakfast in his New York City mansion, Carnegie is said to have perused the morning's *New York Journal*. A headline attracted his attention: "Most Colossal Animal Ever on Earth Just Found Out West!" Accompanying the article was an illustration showing a dinosaur peering into an eleventh-story window of the New York Life Building. Carnegie decided to buy the "colossal animal" and immediately jotted down a note in the newspaper margin. Sent to Dr. William J. Holland, recently appointed director of the new Carnegie Museum, the note read: "Dear Chancellor, Buy this for Pittsburgh." Enclosed with the *Journal* article was a $10,000 check. Holland posthaste set to work to accomplish Carnegie's request.

The discoverer of the dinosaur described in the *Journal* article was William H. Reed, a dinosaur collector and later a staff member of the American Museum. Along with O.C. Marsh, one of the paleontologists mentioned earlier, Reed had also been credited with the discovery of the famous dinosaur quarry at Como Bluff, Wyoming. With such credentials, Reed was the obvious person to contact for the initiation of a dinosaur search, so Holland visited Reed in Wyoming. At this time, Reed explained that while he could find fossils, he knew nothing about preparing or de-

scribing them. With the assurance of an additional crew, Reed signed a year's contract with Carnegie Museum and presented Holland with a single bone from the upper part of a dinosaur limb. Holland thus returned to Pittsburgh with a single bone and a commitment from Reed to find more.

Since the American Museum was in the forefront of dinosaur work, Holland visited the Museum hoping to acquire skilled paleontologists to prepare and describe the fossils Reed was to find. Through Holland's efforts J.L. Wortman, the American Museum's Assistant Curator of Paleontology, was convinced to join Carnegie Museum and there organize a department of paleontology. Also departing in 1899 with Wortman for Carnegie Museum was Arthur S. Coggeshall who would assume responsibility for preparing dinosaur fossils once they were found. Soon after arriving in Pittsburgh, Wortman and Coggeshall boarded the Overland Limited bound for Wyoming.

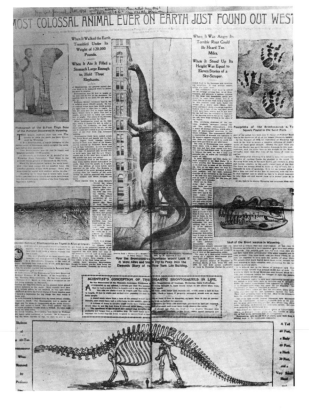

*Top: Reed, working with fossils prepared for shipment from Como Bluff, Wyoming. The dinosaur fossils, after excavation had been wrapped in burlap and plaster and numbered for identification when they arrived in Pittsburgh. Courtesy of American Heritage Center, University of Wyoming. Bottom: Removing fossil bone. An early Section of Vertebrate Fossils staff member painstakingly removes fossil bone from a block of rock.*

*Page 15: Digging up* Diplodocus. *During his visit to "Camp Carnegie" in August, 1899, Dr. Holland examined the* Diplodocus *bones exposed over the past month's work. Holland (foreground) and Dr. Wortman are pictured here uncovering new portions of the* Diplodocus *skeleton.*

At Medicine Bow, Wyoming, the two paleon-tologists were greeted by Reed. Supplies that included a ton of plaster and a bale of burlap (which would be used to wrap and transport large fossil bones) were loaded into a farm wagon drawn by a team of horses. Traveling proved difficult since the crew was faced with rocky terrain and bridges without rails along the sides. Days of wading through streams and pushing the wagon across bridges elapsed before the men reached their destination—the site of Reed's publicized find.

Once on location and with camp set up, Wortman and Coggeshall began digging. After a few days without discovering a single bone, Reed confessed that the dinosaur bone he had given to Holland was the only dinosaur bone he had ever found at the site. Wortman and Coggeshall thus learned that Reed's find of "The Most Colossal Animal" described in the *Journal* article was based upon a single bone.

Although discouraged by Reed's confession, the two men continued their search. Coggeshall writes: "Discouraging? Yes, it was, but bone hunters, like prospectors for gold and silver, have to take discouragement in their stride."[2] And "stride" they did. Two months later, on the afternoon of July 3, 1899, Wortman and Coggeshall found themselves searching for dinosaur fossils thirty miles from the original site. The new location, called Sheep Creek, was chosen because the Morrison Formation, in which big dinosaur fossils were found in other areas, occurred at the surface there.

On the morning of the following day, July 4, a toe bone from a dinosaur's hind foot was uncovered by Coggeshall. By noon, enough of the left pelvis had been cleared so that the men were sure they had made a significant discovery. While it may not have been "The Most Colossal Animal," they knew it was a dinosaur of which Carnegie could be proud. As the skeleton was excavated from the surrounding rock, it became clear that the dinosaur had died in the mud of an ancient lake or stream some 120 million years earlier. Since there had probably been little water movement since the dinosaur's death, the skeleton was practically intact, lying on its right side in much the same position that it likely fell and

died. Although the dinosaur was eventually identified as *Diplodocus* (meaning "double-beamed" in Greek and referring to the fore and aft projections on the chevrons, the small bones on the underside of the tail), Coggeshall suggested that, because of the circumstances and day of its discovery, it might aptly be called the "Star Spangled Dinosaur."

As soon as the importance of the dinosaur discovery was determined, a telegram was sent to Holland, who, in turn, notified Andrew Carnegie. In August, Holland visited the quarry. As news of the find spread, scientists from museums and universities across the country made the trip to "Camp Carnegie," as the headquarters at Sheep Creek was designated.

During the winter, work continued in Pittsburgh. The paleontologists discovered that, although it was the most complete *Diplodocus* ever found up to that time, some of the bones had been weathered away. In the spring of 1900, another field party returned to Camp Carnegie, enlarged the quarry, and uncovered another *Diplodocus* skeleton. The remains collected were included in the composite of *Diplodocus* now standing in Dinosaur Hall.

The composite *Diplodocus* was described in scientific literature in 1901 and, in honor of Carnegie, designated *Diplodocus carnegii*. Measuring 84 feet (25.6 m) long, the skeleton could not have been mounted in Carnegie's museum as it was then. Not until the original Museum building was expanded to its present size did *Diplodocus* stand in Dinosaur Hall.

The weight of "Dippy," as the dinosaur was fondly dubbed by Carnegie's friends, also posed a problem for mounting. In life, Dippy weighed approximately 12 tons (10,886 kg). Although most of the body weight was taken up by flesh rather than bones, the bones, once fossilized, became very heavy. To carry the great weight of the fossilized bones, Coggeshall invented a system for mounting the skeleton. He cast a structural steel framework to support the vertebral column, a method for exhibiting dinosaurs that is still used today in museums throughout the world.

*Left: Pictured with the first* Diplodocus carnegii *cast is Dr. William J. Holland. Above:* Diplodocus carnegii *at the Paris Museum. Dr. Holland (far left) is shown with Arthur S. Coggeshall (third from left, wearing apron) overseeing the installation of the third cast of the dinosaur at the Paris Museum in 1909. Below:* Diplodocus carnegii *at the British Museum. The dinosaur is shown as it appeared following its formal presentation to the British Museum in 1905.*

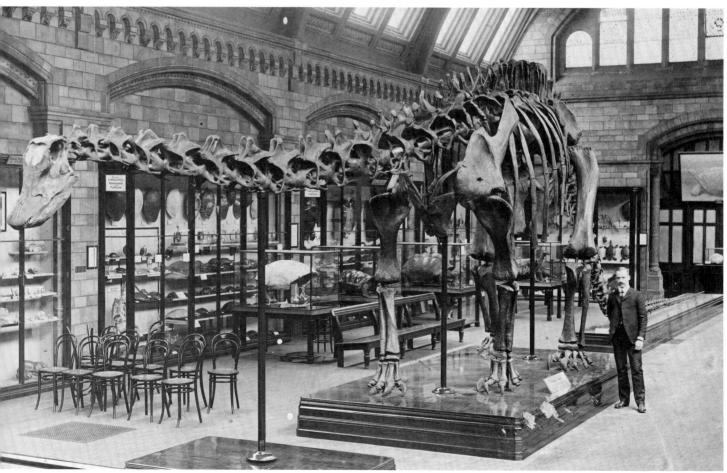

# Celebrity Status for Dippy

The fame of Carnegie's first dinosaur spread quickly. On a visit to Carnegie's Skibo Castle in Scotland, King Edward VII of England noticed a watercolor sketch of Dippy and requested that a duplicate be placed in the British Museum. As one ditty indicates, the King's interest in Dippy sparked similar requests from heads of state throughout the world:

> The Crowned heads of Europe
> All make a royal fuss
> Over Uncle Andy
> And his old *Diplodocus*.[3]

For two years, a crew of Italian plasterers skilled in casting statuary made molds of the *Diplodocus* skeleton. Working with such heavy yet fragile bones made the task tedious, but in anticipation of future requests, the crew produced five replicas in addition to the one requested by King Edward. Once complete, the first cast was disassembled, crated and shipped to the British Museum. Under Coggeshall's direction, the *Diplodocus* cast was reassembled in London. Finally, in 1905, the cast was formally presented by Carnegie to the Trustees of the British Museum—one of which was the King.

With Dippy's continuing fame, requests for casts came from Kaiser Wilhelm of Germany, President Fallieres of France, Emperor Franz Josef of Austria, and King Vittorio Emmanuele III of Italy. For each request, casts of Dippy were sent to the respective museums, a Carnegie Museum crew oversaw the reassembling of the skeleton, and Holland formally presented the replicas to the heads of state. Holland was, in turn, honored and decorated by each country aforementioned.

With five replicas housed in European museums, Holland had visions of future royal requests and arranged for the casting of four additional skeletons. In 1910, members of the Carnegie Museum staff and Holland traveled to Russia to assemble and present one of these replicas to Czar Nicholas II. From there they traveled to Spain at the request of King Alfonso XIII. The next trip was to South America. At Argentina's National Museum, a replica of

*Diplodocus* was formally presented to President Rogue Saenz Peña. Negotiations for the remaining cast were initiated in 1928 by President Emilio Portes Gil of Mexico, and the presentation to the Mexican National Museum occurred a year later.

In 1934, a final replica of Dippy was made. Carnegie Museum sent the cast to the Bayerische Staatssammlung für Paläontologie in Munich, Germany, in exchange for a large number of European fossils. The *Diplodocus* replica was not mounted when it arrived, and, during World War II, records for the replica were lost. In 1977, the replica was discovered in the Museum's storerooms, still in its original thirty-three crates.

Although the last *Diplodocus* replica was sent abroad in 1934, the molds continued to travel throughout the United States. In 1957, the molds were shipped to the Field House of Natural History near Dinosaur National Monument in Vernal, Utah. A replica was prepared, and today Dippy stands on the Museum's lawn. From Utah, the molds were sent to Rocky Mount Children's Museum in North Carolina and the new Houston Museum of Natural Science in Texas. Unfortunately, by the time they reached Texas, the molds had disintegrated with use and age. Thus, instead of casting a replica, the Houston Museum acquired the partial skeleton of a small *Diplodocus* that had been excavated by Carnegie Museum. Today, this restored and mounted *Diplodocus* skeleton stands in the Houston Museum's central rotunda.

# Earl Douglass and the Utah Dinosaur Quarry

Dippy was the first of a long parade of dinosaurs that found their way into Carnegie Museum. Most of these dinosaurs were excavated at a single quarry today known as Dinosaur National Monument. Situated in northeastern Utah on the southern flank of the Uinta Mountains, the quarry is 320 feet (97.5 m) long and 50 feet (15.2 m) wide. It overlooks a spectacular canyon cut through the mountains by the Green River, and the rocks at

*Left: Earl Douglass, discoverer of Dinosaur National Monument. During the thirteen years Douglass worked for Carnegie Museum at the quarry, some 350 tons of dinosaur bones and other fossils were shipped back to Pittsburgh for study and exhibit. Douglass' repeated urgings contributed to the eventual construction of a unique museum at Dinosaur National Monument.*
*Above left: Earl Douglass with bones of* Diplodocus *(Smithsonian specimen) about 1923. Courtesy of U.S. Department of the Interior, National Park Service.*
*Above right: The Douglass cabin; photograph taken 1944 or 1945. Green River in the background. Courtesy of the U.S. Department of the Interior, National Park Service.*

this quarry are tipped up at a 67° angle, exposing a massive accumulation of dinosaur remains.

In September, 1908, while accompanying Holland on a tour of the area, Earl Douglass, a new paleontologist for the Museum, discovered an indication of the quarry's wealth. Earlier in the year, Holland had learned from other scientists that this particular area contained rocks of the Morrison Formation dating back to a time when dinosaurs roamed the land. While visiting Douglass at a nearby work site where he was collecting fossil mammals, Holland disclosed this information. The next morning, the two men set out in search of dinosaurs. After two days of scouring the desolate, rocky area, Douglass happened upon a weathered dinosaur thigh bone lying at the bottom of a narrow ravine. The bone appeared as though it had eroded out of one of the ravine's rock layers. Such a find was enough to convince Holland and Douglass that the area was worth more prospecting.

The following spring, outfitted and accompanied by an assistant, Douglass set out for northeastern Utah to find the rock stratum holding the rest of the dinosaur bones. Day after day, the two men searched the area. Through the ever-increasing heat of spring and summer, they scrambled, slipped and climbed over the rugged terrain. Finally, on August 17, almost at the point of despair, as Douglass walked along a dry wash, he saw scraps of fossilized bone. His heart leaped as he followed the bone outcropping up the rocky edge of a jagged saw-toothed ridge. There, in the sandstone ledge, he discovered eight dinosaur tail vertebrate still joined together in the exact position they had occupied in a living animal. Four days later, Douglass wrote to Carnegie Museum saying: "I have discovered a huge Dinosaur,... and if the skeleton is as perfect as the portions we have exposed, the task of excavating will be enormous and will cost a lot of money, but the rock is the kind to get perfect bones.... If it should continue as it has begun it would be the best Jurassic Dinosaur in existence....Carnegie wanted a Dinosaur for the king of England. If he wants one now there is a fair show that we have it."[4]

With each day's work, more of the dinosaur skeleton was uncovered. Young farmers and ranchers from neighboring communities were hired and trained to help to remove the fossilized dinosaur bones, but the progress was still slow. Douglass and his crew had difficulty drilling through the extremely hard sandstone encasing the skeleton. As the sparks flew, the chisels soon became dull. The 25 mile (40 km) trip by team and wagon to Vernal, the nearest town to the quarry, to pick up supplies and new equipment also impeded the progress. In an attempt to remedy this obstacle to the completion of the project, a forge was set up at the site of the excavation and steel was ordered. The quickly accumulating rubble also became too much to handle, so a team of horses was hired to haul the rubble away. Some time later, a railroad and mine cars were installed to dispose of the vast amounts of waste stone.

In the fall, Mrs. Pearl Douglass and the couple's year-old child joined Douglass who, with his crew, continued excavating long into the winter while Mrs. Douglass served as the cook. Dr. Holland received a letter from Douglass describing the conditions he was working under during the winter of 1909:

> We are having extremely cold weather here now. I do not think that the thermometer gets up to zero except in sheltered sunshine. It has been as low as 3° Fahr. [Fahrenheit]. I cannot very well work around bones with paste and plaster [materials used to protect bones during transport] as it freezes immediately, but we can go on with the excavating and sinking down nearly as well as ever if you can get giant powder [dynamite].[5]

As more of the skeleton was uncovered, the hope that an entire dinosaur would be found increased. The tail bones were found to continue in both directions with only slight displacement of the vertebrae from their natural positions. When fully uncovered, this skeleton, found to be that of *Apatosaurus,* was of exceptional size and completeness. Although the very tip of the tail was missing, sixty-four successive tail vertebrae were found, more than twice the number ever discovered up to that time. The completeness of the skeleton was unprecedented in many other respects. The only missing parts, in fact, were the

left hind leg, right hind foot, the right forearm and foot, the tip of the tail, the sternum, and possibly (see later) the skull.

Named *Apatosaurus louisae* in honor of Mrs. Andrew (Louise) Carnegie, the skeleton was mounted for display at Carnegie Museum. Measuring 71½ feet (21.8 m) long and standing 15 feet (4.6 m) tall at the arch of the back, the skeleton represented the most perfect of the four mounted specimens in the country. While bones from another dinosaur of a similar size and age completed the *Apatosaurus* mount, the skeleton remained headless. Although a dinosaur skull was found during the excavation of *Apatosaurus,* it was not certain that the skull belonged to the dinosaur. Because of a debate with Osborn (the director of the American Museum of Natural History in New York) over the shape of the *Apatosaurus* skull, Holland instructed Douglass to find a skull still attached to *Apatosaurus'* neck bones so that certainty could be established. Although Douglass continued this search until 1922, the dispute over *Apatosaurus'* true skull was not settled during Holland's lifetime. (For more on this matter of heads, see pages 71-73.)

Before Douglass completely uncovered *Apatosaurus,* he hit upon another dinosaur almost as big. In the midst of excavating the second dinosaur, the men found a third. Douglass described this find in a letter to Holland: "It is almost certain now that we have two big Dinosaurs together instead of one.... Besides this there is the skeleton of a small Dinosaur. We are certainly in luck, I never have heard of 'the likes of this'...."[6]

A few years after Douglass' initial discovery, the land around the dinosaur quarry was thrown open to homesteading. In order to prevent a speculator from filing claim on the quarry property, Holland instructed Douglass to file a claim for mineral rights to the land on behalf of Carnegie Museum. Although the government initially disallowed the claim on the basis that dinosaur bones cannot be considered minerals in the usual sense, the ruling was appealed. Holland traveled to Washington, D.C., and conferred with his old friend Dr. Charles D. Walcott, Secretary of the Smithsonian Institution and former director of the U.S. Geological Survey. As a paleontologist

*Above:* Welding supports for Apatosaurus louisae. *Taken around 1915, this picture illustrates the technique developed by preparator Arthur S. Coggeshall for mounting dinosaur skeletons. The enormous weight of the fossilized vertebral column was supported by a steel framework.* **Top left:** *Crating dinosaur bones at Carnegie Quarry. In order to reach fossil bones, many tons of surrounding rock must first be removed. This photo from 1911 shows an accumulation of discarded waste rock at the Quarry.* **Bottom left:** *Looking east through the Quarry cut, showing "muck cart" and tracks; plastered and partially crated fossils in foreground. Hanging on a line over the cut are burlap strips torn from used bags from the nearby gilsonite mines; the strips were used in jacketing the bones. Grid lines painted on the cliff to aid in plotting fossil locations are visible at left. Courtesy of U.S. Department of the Interior, National Park Service.*

of international repute, Walcott recognized the timeliness and importance of Holland's concern and convinced President Woodrow Wilson of the significance of the matter. On October 14, 1915, President Wilson signed an order designating the eighty acres surrounding the quarry a national monument. Holland explained the transaction to Douglass:

> Under date of January the 8th I have received from the Secretary of the Interior a permit allowing the Carnegie Museum to carry on the work of investigation at our quarry now designated as the "Dinosaur National Monument" for the year 1916; and for your further full information I am having a copy of the letter of the Secretary made, which I herewith transmit to you.
>
> You will observe that at the expiration of the year 1916 an application from us to continue our work will be considered and so on from time to time until we may finally adjudge that it is no longer expedient for us to carry on our work in that spot.[7]

With Carnegie Museum periodically filing application for permission to excavate the quarry, Douglass and his crew continued to uncover dinosaur after dinosaur for thirteen years. The work persisted year-round through the blistering heat of summer and the sub-zero temperatures of winter. By 1922, 446 crates of fossils weighing a total of 700,000 pounds (317,520 kg) had been shipped to Carnegie Museum. Contained within the find were twenty mountable skeletons representing ten dinosaur species as well as many isolated bones and partial skeletons.

Throughout the thirteen years of working the quarry at Dinosaur National Monument, transporting the bones to Carnegie Museum in Pittsburgh was a major undertaking. Four-horse teams hauled high-wheeled freight wagons filled with the crates of bones over sixty miles (96.6 km) of rutted roads to the nearest rail lines at Dragon, Utah. There, the crates were loaded into boxcars of the now-defunct Uintah Railway. From this narrow-gauge railway they were transported to the standard-guage Denver and Rio Grande line and then on to Pittsburgh.

# The Halt of Collecting

With Andrew Carnegie's death in 1919, funds for dinosaur collecting began to dwindle. Back at Carnegie Museum, the staff of preparators was hard pressed to keep up with the continuous flow of fossils from the Dinosaur National Monument quarry and the field expeditions in Wyoming and Montana. Storage space was also becoming scarce. Influenced by such factors, Carnegie Museum decided to cease operations at the quarry in Utah.

Despite Douglass' plea for more time, Carnegie Museum's operations at Dinosaur National Monument ended sometime in late 1922 through early 1923. Encouraged by Douglass' belief that as many as three dinosaur skeletons still remained to be uncovered, Carnegie Museum informed the Smithsonian Institution of the richness of the quarry. During the summer of 1923, a paleontologist and crew from the Smithsonian collected fossil bones including a *Diplodocus* skeleton from the site. The *Diplodocus* skeleton is now on exhibit at the Smithsonian.

During this same year, Douglass was asked by the University of Utah to supervise dinosaur collecting in the area. Under his direction, the best *Allosaurus* skeleton ever collected was found. In addition to these fossilized bones, partial skeletons of five other dinosaurs were shipped to Salt Lake City.

In 1924 the University of Utah completed its work in the dinosaur quarry; still, Dinosaur National Monument was not abandoned. In signing his agreement, President Wilson indicated that Dinosaur National Monument should eventually become an exhibit of dinosaur bones for the public. No one is sure who first conceived the idea for such a display, but Earl Douglass recorded it in his diary as early as 1915. And it was Douglass who brought this idea to the attention of Charles Walcott in 1923:

> The number of visitors here has increased from year to year and the popularity of the monument will undoubtedly grow rapidly in the future as people hear of it and learn where it is. The greater number come in the

*Work continues today at Dinosaur National Monument where visitors have the opportunity to watch pre-parators expose bones embedded in the "wall of dinosaurs." Courtesy of U.S. Department of the Interior, National Park Service.*

tourist season from June to October. Last August there were over 500 visitors to the quarry. They came from early morning to dark—in fact some have "viewed the remains" by flash light.

I hope—and there are thousands of others—that the government, for the benefit of science and the people, will uncover a large area, leave the bones and skeletons in relief and house them in. It would make one of the most astounding and instructive sights imaginable.[8]

Periodically, over the next thirty years, attempts were made to prepare Dinosaur National Monument for public viewing. In 1953, Dr. Theodore E. White was placed in charge of the scientific aspects of the project. White selected an unworked section of the original quarry for further excavation. Although initially few dinosaur bones were found, digging continued until a deeper layer containing a wealth of dinosaur bones was reached—the same layer of rock as the one in which Douglass originally "struck it rich."

In 1958, a unique building of steel, glass and concrete was opened to the public. One entire wall of the structure is, in actuality, the 183 feet (55.8 m) long and 60 feet (18 m) high sandstone cliff from which dinosaurs continue to be uncovered. At the Monument, visitors today have the opportunity to watch preparators as they continue to expose the bones imbedded in the "wall of dinosaurs." Thus far, over a thousand dinosaur bones representing at least eight distinct types have been found in the wall. Rare and significant specimens such as a baby *Stegosaurus* (one of only two ever found), the partial skeleton of a particularly large *Camarasaurus,* and previously undiscovered bones of other dinosaurs that provided important clues to their appearance are included as Monument discoveries.

Douglass' wish has, thus, finally come to fruition. As dinosaur bones continue to be discovered, they will be left in place exactly as they were buried millions of years ago. At Dinosaur National Monument they will be treated with the awe and respect deserved by such ancient remnants of early life. Also, the Monument serves as a tribute to men such as Carnegie, Holland, Douglass, and White who had the foresight, persistence and patience to develop what has become the greatest of dinosaur deposits. Perhaps phrases of Douglass best captured the testimonial: "It is fitting...that we should remember each other as we worked together as pioneers and few will appreciate the work that we did except ourselves.... Yet it seems I could not do otherwise. There is something beyond our own wills that leads us on and if we do not submit to it life is a failure."[9]

# Dinosaur Collecting Today

With the initial request sent to Holland for dinosaurs in 1898, Carnegie enclosed a check for $10,000. Throughout the next nineteen years, Carnegie donated more than $250,000 to Carnegie Museum specifically for collecting, preparing and studying dinosaurs and other fossil vertebrates. In April 1917, two years before his death, Carnegie discontinued his private funding and requested that the Trustees assume the payment of paleontological research out of a general fund. With this diminishing of support, Carnegie Museum's involvement with dinosaurs gradually declined, and field parties became more concerned with fossil mammals from the Cenozoic, the era following the Age of Reptiles.

Nonetheless, dinosaur research continues. Carnegie Museum of Natural History's dinosaurs are being studied and described today by dinosaur experts including Dr. David S. Berman, Associate Curator of Vertebrate Fossils at the Museum and Dr. John McIntosh, a dinosaur specialist and professor of physics at Wesleyan University in Connecticut. Dr. Berman currently heads up a field project to collect early forms of dinosaurs from the Triassic at Ghost Ranch Quarry, New Mexico. To date, he and his associates have uncovered and are preparing a phytosaur skull; they are also uncovering numerous *Coelophysis* skeletons. (Phytosaurs are a group of Triassic reptiles very crocodile-like in appearance; *Coelophysis* is typical of early Triassic dinosaurs.) Because Carnegie Museum of Natural History's collection

did not include a Triassic dinosaur, the work is particularly significant. Once the newly uncovered specimens are prepared and displayed, Carnegie Museum's Dinosaur Hall will provide a more complete picture of the Age of Reptiles.

As is evident in the following chapters, there is no shortage of unanswered questions about dinosaurs for scientists to investigate. Some of the answers, in fact, are hidden on storage racks. For example, to this day, some bones shipped to Carnegie Museum of Natural History from Dinosaur National Monument have yet to be unpacked from their original shipping crates and removed from their rocky surroundings. Because the task of freeing bones from the surrounding rock is even more tedious than the actual removal of the heavy blocks of bone-rich sandstone from quarries, some specimens collected decades ago have never been studied by a specialist. In an attempt to "catch up"—or to save traveling time and aggravation—many dinosaur students do their prospecting on the dusty storage racks of the older museums.

These storage racks are a major concern of any dinosaur-collecting museum. First, they house the specimens not on exhibit; interestingly these specimens greatly outnumber the mounted skeletons in all research collections. Secondly, the storage racks must be capable of supporting the extremely heavy weight of the fossil bones. These bones must be protected from breakage and disintegration as a result of such factors as hot, dry, dirt-laden air. When damage occurs, the bones must be repaired. A museum's stewardship over these priceless prehistoric relics never ends.

Today, Carnegie Museum of Natural History owns approximately 500 catalogued dinosaur specimens. Topped only by the American Museum of Natural History and the National Museum of Natural History (Smithsonian Institution), Carnegie Museum has probably the third largest overall dinosaur collection in the United States. The collection ranges from nearly complete skeletons to some catalogued specimens that are single bones. Five of the Museum's dinosaur specimens are *types*—remains that have been selected by a paleontologist as the basis for naming a new species. Parts of several skeletons have been sent to other museums in the United States

*Top:* Uncovering the Coelophysis *skeleton. Associate Curator Dr. David S. Berman and Preparator Allen D. McCrady, both of Carnegie Museum's Section of Vertebrate Fossils, are shown removing this relatively small dinosaur from surrounding rock.* *Bottom:* Pictured with Curatorial Assistant Amy C. Henrici is but a sampling of the over 40,000 catalogued items in the collections of the Section of Vertebrate Fossils at Carnegie Museum of Natural History.

*Page 25:* Restoration of Coelophysis, *a small, bipedal theropod dinosaur from the Triassic. Carnegie Museum expeditions led by Dr. David S. Berman have recently excavated remains of this dinosaur from a quarry in Triassic rocks at Ghost Ranch, New Mexico. Courtesy of the Pennsylvania Historical and Museum Commission—William Penn Memorial Museum.*

for exhibition.

Of those dinosaurs on display in Dinosaur Hall, seven are representative of the Jurassic Period (212 to 143 million years ago). Despite the fact that many of these dinosaurs were found in different states, many were found in the same formation, the Morrison. *Diplodocus* and *Apatosaurus,* for example, although found in Wyoming and Utah respectively, are both taken from the Morrison Formation, which dates back to the late Jurassic Period.

Dinosaur Hall's remaining four dinosaurs are taken from rock formations laid down during the Cretaceous Period (135 to 70 million years ago). Only one of the Cretaceous dinosaurs on display, *Triceratops,* was collected by a Museum paleontologist. The others were obtained from other museums in exchange for other fossils.

## The Bayet Collection

Forms of life other than dinosaurs are also displayed in Dinosaur Hall. These include a variety of animals that roamed the earth, swam in the seas, or flew in the air during the Mesozoic Era. Many of these other representatives of life in the Mesozoic Era came to Carnegie Museum of Natural History through purchase of an extensive fossil collection in 1903.

This huge collection was amassed by one man, Baron Ernest de Bayet of Brussels, Belgium. Bayet, who spent forty years collecting what was at that time one of the largest private collections of fossils in western Europe, served as Secretary to Belgium's King Leopold II for many years. Bayet stored his massive collection in a house. In fact, almost every room except one small bedroom of his three-story house was crammed with the collection. Some speculate that the Baron did not actually live in the house but was forced to provide a separate house for the collection. In any case, in 1898, it took an official from the British Museum (Natural History) five days to make an inventory of the collection.

When Bayet was about sixty-five-years-old, he married a woman much younger than himself. In order to gratify her wish for a small chalet on the shores of Lake Como in northern Italy, Bayet found it necessary to raise additional money. He thus decided to sell his fossil collection.

Carnegie Museum of Natural History learned of the availability of the Bayet Collection in October of 1902. A German dealer sent the Museum's Curator of Paleontology, J.B. Hatcher, a notice that Bayet wanted to sell "his most celebrated and most precious collection"[10] of fossils. Hatcher appealed to Carnegie Museum's director, Dr. W.J. Holland, to arrange for the purchase.

In an enthusiastic letter written on May 9, 1903, to Andrew Carnegie at his retirement home Skibo, in Scotland, Holland told Carnegie that the collection was for sale. "We are doing such splendid things in American paleontology that I should like very much to secure the collection which, added to what we are securing and will secure in years to come, will make our Museum one of the Gibraltars of paleontological science in the world."[11] He emphasized the need for haste in arranging to purchase it since the Imperial Museum of St. Petersburg, London's British Museum, Harvard University, and the American Museum of Natural History were also eager to acquire it. Purchase price for the collection was set at $25,000.

On May 22, 1903, Mr. Carnegie granted permission to buy the Bayet Collection in its entirety. Holland was delighted, writing his thanks to Mr. Carnegie: "Upon my return I find your letter, which convinces me that there is efficacy in prayer, provided the prayer be addressed to the right person. Your most gracious consent to purchase the Baron de Bayet collection at Brussels has made me very happy, and when Mr. Hatcher, who is out in the wilds of Montana, hears of it, I think that he will for once lose his quiet dignity and go out into the sage-brush and turn a handspring."[12]

The final price paid to the Baron for the collection, $20,500, covered the packing and shipping of the fossils. Holland went by ship to Brussels to oversee the packing of the collection, reporting in a letter to Mr. Carnegie's secretary that, "I never worked harder in my life."[13] While he was packing, Holland took the time to prepare a sketchbook of the baron's home, including information needed for reassembling the skeletons

*Ground floor of Baron de Bayet's residence including the Coach House. This sketch was made by Dr. W.J. Holland in July 1903 while Holland inventoried Bayet's vast collection of fossils. Holland's notes indicate that fossils were stuffed in every available space.*

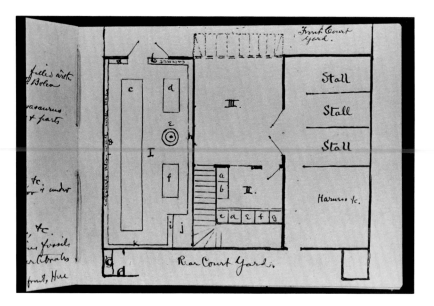

when they reached Pittsburgh.

All 259 cases of the Bayet Collection arrived in Pittsburgh in September, 1903. Because of the lack of adequate space in what was then the Museum, the collection was sent to a warehouse for storage. Shortly after, a fire in the warehouse endangered the collection; fortunately, although the cases were dampened, their contents were not damaged. After completion of the present Carnegie Institute building, the collection was moved to Carnegie Museum of Natural History. Except for the portion exhibited in Dinosaur Hall, the collection is stored in the Section of Vertebrate Fossils and the Section of Invertebrate Fossils.

Mr. Carnegie's purchase was an invaluable addition and complement to the Museum's growing collections of North American fossils. The Collection, whose individual specimens number in the tens of thousands, is especially rich in invertebrates from the Paleozoic, Mesozoic, and Cenozoic Eras of Europe. Many specimens from individual localities are irreplaceable because the collecting sites from which they came have either been destroyed, filled in, or are obscured by urban sprawl.

Dr. John L. Carter, current Curator of Invertebrate Fossils at Carnegie Museum of Natural History, learned this information the hard way. In 1971, before joining Carnegie Museum, Carter visited Belgium hoping to collect brachiopods and molluscs from the famous old quarries at Vise

and Tournai. To his dismay, the quarries had been ruined for fossil collecting. When he came to Carnegie Museum the following year, Carter was pleasantly surprised to find several thousand fossils from these sites in the Bayet Collection.

The Bayet Collection includes superb Jurassic invertebrates from the quarries at Solnhofen and nearby sites in southern Germany. Preserved on yellowish-white, fine-grained limestone slabs, some show impressions of soft parts that are rarely seen in fossils: dragon-flies with out-stretched wings; prawns and lobster- and crab-like crustaceans with legs and delicate antennae exquisitely preserved; and squids and cuttlefish with the outlines of the tentacles, their ink sacs still containing ink. Several specimens of this Collection, which is probably the largest collection of Solnhofen invertebrates in North America, can be seen in Dinosaur Hall.

The Collection also includes many fish, several of which are displayed in Dinosaur Hall. The skeletons of reptiles that lived in shallow seas that covered parts of Europe during the Mesozoic Era can be seen along one wall of Dinosaur Hall as well. Another priceless part of the Bayet Collection, the pterosaurs ("winged reptiles"), consists of eleven specimens. Four of these are displayed along the back wall of Dinosaur Hall. These fossils are especially valuable since only about one pterosaur per year on the average has been recovered over the past two-hundred years from two of the limestone quarries in Germany, and only about twenty have been collected from a third early Jurassic one. With these eleven pterosaurs, Carnegie Museum has the fourth largest collection of Jurassic pterosaurs in the world, outranked only by museums in Munich, Eichstätt, and London.

# What is a Dinosaur?

About 300 million years ago, in the late Paleozoic, the first reptiles appeared, and from them evolved the dinosaurs and other reptiles, the birds, and the mammals. These ancient reptiles had a broad skull with a solid roof except for openings for the eyes and nostrils. In those reptiles that eventually gave rise to mammals, an additional opening developed in the cheek region of the skull. A second lineage of reptiles ancestral to dinosaurs and birds evolved two openings in the cheek region, a condition termed *diapsid.* By the beginning of the Triassic, some diapsids had developed a third pair of openings on their skulls in front of their eyes and another on the lower jaws. Both openings reduced the weight of the skull with little loss of strength.

A further reduction of bones occurred in the hip and shoulder regions of the archosaurs, a subgroup of diapsid reptiles that included the dinosaurs. With this reduction, the short, stubby legs that sprawled out sideways, typical of most other reptiles and amphibians, were moved under the body. This leg position increased support and efficiency of movement; these diapsids could run faster with less effort, and, as certain modern-day lizards, could run on their hind legs. Eventually, diapsids developed hind legs larger and more powerful than the forelegs and became bipedal.

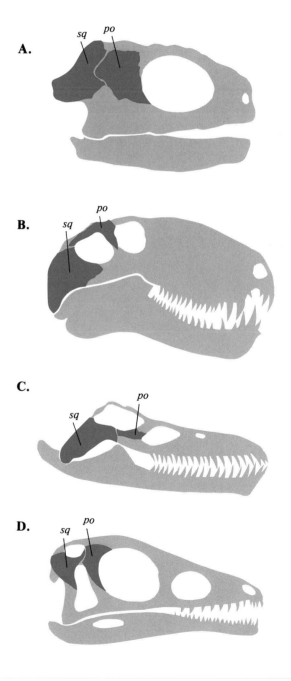

*The four basic skull patterns found in reptiles.*
*A. Anapsid Condition. In this skull pattern there are no openings in the temporal region. This condition is found in both fossil and living turtles.*
*B. Synapsid Condition. In this skull pattern a single temporal opening is bounded above by the postorbital and squamosal bones. Synapsid reptiles, such as* Dimetrodon *pictured here, gave rise to mammals.*
*C. Euryapsid Condition. In this skull pattern the single temporal opening is bounded below by the postorbital and squamosal bones. This skull pattern occurred in the now-extinct plesiosaurs (pictured here) and nothosaurs.*
*D. Diapsid Condition. Two temporal openings are present in this skull pattern. The postorbital and squamosal bones meet between these two openings. All archosaurs, such as the dinosaur* Compsognathus *represented here, as well as lizards, snakes and their fossil relatives are diapsid reptiles.*

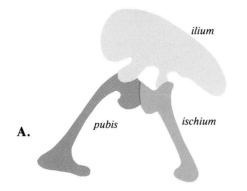

A.

These active, bipedal reptiles are called *thecodonts* (Latin for "socket-toothed") because their teeth are embedded in sockets in the jaws. Thecodonts became extinct at the close of the Triassic, but their descendants, especially the dinosaurs, became the dominant land vertebrates during the rest of the Mesozoic Era.

From their inception dinosaurs were distinguishable on the basis of hip structure as two orders: Saurischians, such as *Diplodocus,* have a pelvic structure similar to that of lizards and other reptiles; ornithischians, such as *Triceratops,* have a pelvis somewhat like that in birds.

*The two basic types of pelvic structure found in dinosaurs. Three bones make up the pelvis or hip of the dinosaur. Position and orientation of these three bones distinguish the two major groups of dinosaurs.*
*A. The pelvic structure of saurischian dinosaurs. Like most other reptiles, in saurischians the pubis and ischium each extend down from the ilium, with the pubis slanting forward and the ischium projecting backward.*
*B. The pelvic structure of ornithischian dinosaurs. In the ornithischian dinosaurs, the ilium is in the same position. The pubis, however, has become two-pronged: one prong is parallel to the ischium and the new prong extends forward. This pelvic structure is similar to that found in birds.*

B.

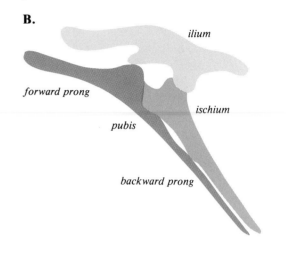

*Coelophysis*
*Compsognathus*

**Coelurosaurs**

*Albertosaurus*
*Allosaurus*
*Ceratosaurus*
*Megalosaurus*
*Tyrannosaurus*

**Carnosaurs**

*Plateosaurus*

**Prosauropods**

*Apatosaurus*
*Barosaurus*
*Brachiosaurus*
*Camarasaurus*
*Cetiosaurus*
*Diplodocus*
*Hypselosaurus*

**Sauropods**

**THEROPODS**

**SAUROPODOMORPHS**

**SAURISCHIANS**

The order Saurischia can be divided into two groups: the carnivorous, bipedal theropods; and the herbivorous, quadrupedal sauropodomorphs. Theropods, being carnivorous, were usually equipped with sharp, pointed teeth for seizing their prey. They had bird-like feet and hollow limb bones.

The theropods include a number of large, heavily built flesh-eaters, two of which, *Tyrannosaurus* and *Allosaurus,* are present in Dinosaur Hall. These theropods had big heads and wide mouths to accomodate their principal weapons—their great, curved teeth. Their necks were short to support the weight of their big heads; their forelegs and hands were relatively small. These large theropods almost certainly preyed upon the large plant-eating dinosaurs.

Other theropods were small, slightly built, predaceous animals, some roughly the size of a human. The smallest full-grown dinosaur is the theropod *Compsognathus* that lived during the late Jurassic. It grew to be only approximately 20-24 inches (50-60 cm) long. Other small theropods were specialized in various ways: Some had an enlarged, slashing inner toe on the hind foot; others were somewhat ostrich-like in stature.

*The evolution and classification of the major groups of saurischian dinosaurs.*

*Below: The evolution and classification of the major groups of ornithischian dinosaurs.*

The second group in the order Saurischia, the plant-eating sauropodomorphs, were considerably larger and heavier than the theropods. The sauropodomorphs are sub-divided into two major groups called infraorders: the prosauropods and the sauropods. Prosauropods, the best-known example of which is *Plateosaurus,* are known to have existed only in the late Triassic. The sauropods appeared during the Jurassic. Unlike the earlier prosauropods, the sauropods had long necks and tails and were strictly quadrupedal. Although the name "sauropod" means "lizard-footed," the feet of sauropods actually were modified for weight support, somewhat resembling those of modern elephants and rhinoceroses. The late Jurassic sauropods—*Diplodocus, Apatosaurus,* and *Camarasaurus*—are displayed in Dinosaur Hall.

All other dinosaurs belong to the order Ornithischia, which contains four subgroups, three of which are represented at Carnegie Museum. In addition to their bird-like pelvis, most ornithischians had no teeth in the front of their mouths. Instead, they probably had horny beaks. With one known exception all were plant-eaters. Members of the first and earliest subgroup, ornithopods, usually were bipedal, although many of them probably dropped to all four feet occasionally. *Dryosaurus, Camptosaurus,* and *Corythosaurus* were ornithopods.

The remaining three subgroups of ornithischians were descended from ornithopods. All dinosaurs in these three subgroups lost the ability to walk solely on their hind legs. Despite this four-footed posture, however, representatives of these subgroups had hind legs that were noticeably longer than their forelegs. They were further characterized by their protective armor.

One such subgroup appearing during the Jurassic is Stegosauria of which familiar *Stegosaurus* is a member. As is evident from the *Stegosaurus* skeleton displayed in the Museum's Dinosaur Hall, the stegosaurs had various combinations of upright plates and spines on the shoulders, along the backbone, and on the tail.

Ankylosaurs, another subgroup of ornithischians, were almost completely encased in an armor of bony plates. Spines and club-like tails provided further protection for these dinosaurs that appeared in the Cretaceous. Unfortunately, no ankylosaurs are exhibited in Dinosaur Hall.

The last ornithischian subgroup, the horned dinosaurs or ceratopsians, were the last dinosaurs to evolve. They appeared during the Cretaceous and survived until the final extinction of all dinosaurs at the close of the Mesozoic Era. Even though they were latecomers, the ceratopsians were common in both North America and eastern Asia.

The ceratopsians were characterized by a protective shield of bone and skin that extended over the back of the neck. One or more horns protruded from their horny shield. *Protoceratops* and *Triceratops,* two ceratopsians, can be seen in Dinosaur Hall. *Protoceratops* was one of the earliest and smallest known ceratopsians; *Triceratops* was one the the latest and largest.

Stegosaurus

**STEGOSAURS**

Ankylosaurus

**ANKYLOSAURS**

Protoceratops
Torosaurus
Triceratops

**CERATOPSIANS**

Anatosaurus
Camptosaurus
Corythosaurus
Dryosaurus
Hadrosaurus
Hypsilophodon
Iguanodon
Trachodon

**ORNITHOPODS**

**ORNITHISCHIANS**

*Evolutionary tree and fossil record of the major groups of archosaurs. The width of the shaded areas indicates the diversity of each group during its geologic time range.*

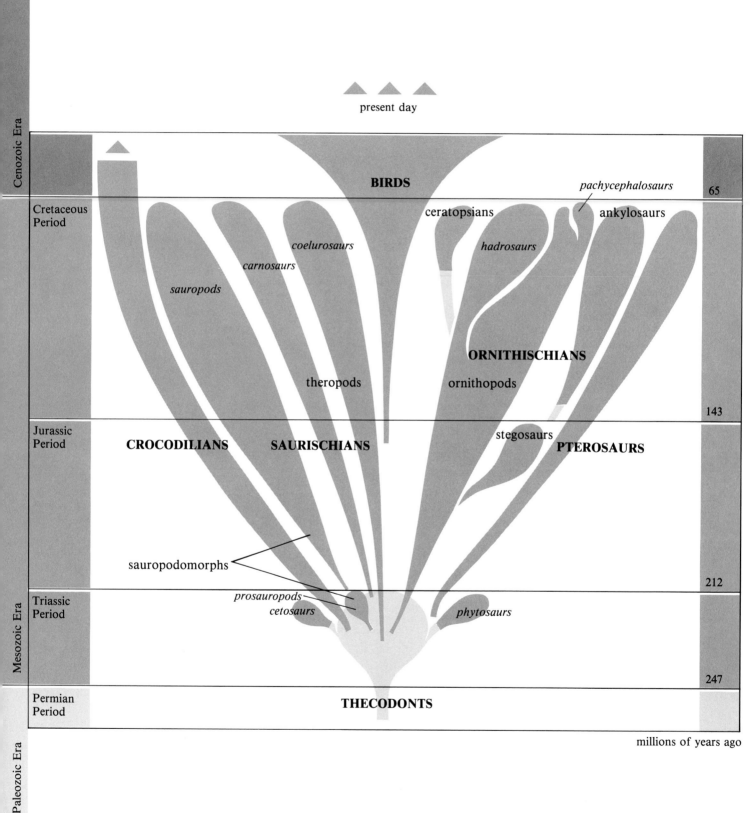

present day

Cenozoic Era

Paleozoic Era

Mesozoic Era

BIRDS

*pachycephalosaurs*

ceratopsians

ankylosaurs

Cretaceous
Period

*coelurosaurs*

*hadrosaurs*

*carnosaurs*

*sauropods*

ORNITHISCHIANS

theropods

ornithopods

65

143

Jurassic
Period

stegosaurs

CROCODILIANS

SAURISCHIANS

PTEROSAURS

sauropodomorphs

212

Triassic
Period

*prosauropods*

*cetosaurs*

*phytosaurs*

247

Permian
Period

THECODONTS

millions of years ago

30

# Were the Dinosaurs Warm~Blooded?

Living reptiles are cold-blooded, but were the dinosaurs as well? Were dinosaurs reptiles whose metabolism and activity levels rose and fell with the temperature of their surroundings? Or were dinosaurs alert, warm-blooded creatures capable of maintaining a constant body temperature under a wide range of environmental conditions?

There is no direct evidence, but several lines of speculation suggest that some dinosaurs may have been as alert and responsive as the warm-blooded birds or mammals of our world.

Whether an animal is cold-blooded (an ectotherm) or warm-blooded (an endotherm) depends upon two things: first, the extent of its ability to distribute oxygen efficiently to its body cells and, second, its power to regulate and maintain the heat generated by its metabolic processes.

Living reptiles, with the exception of the crocodilians, have a relatively primitive oxygen distribution system—a three-chambered heart—that limits the amount of oxygen that can be circulated at any one time. Birds and mammals, on the other hand, have evolved a highly efficient four-chambered heart capable of circulating more richly oxygenated blood. Animals with four-chambered hearts are able to metabolize at a faster rate, thereby producing more heat and energy, because their rate of oxygen utilization can be maintained at a higher level.

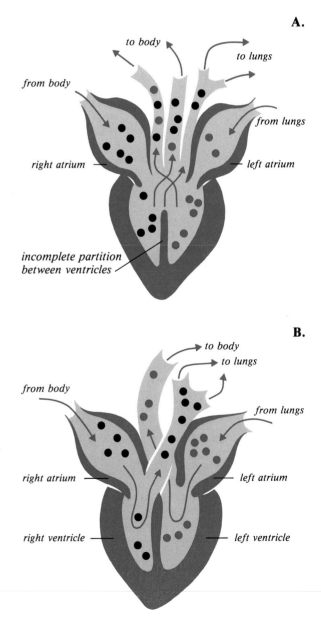

A.

B.

A typical reptilian three-chambered heart and mammalian four-chambered heart.
A. A typical reptilian three-chambered heart. In the reptilian heart, the two halves of the ventricle are not completely divided so that blood returning from the body with Carbon Dioxide ($CO_2$) and from the lungs with Oxygen ($O_2$) undergo some mixing before being pumped to the body.
B. A typical mammalian four-chambered heart. The mammalian heart, with two completely separated ventricles, avoids any mixing of blood returning from the body with Carbon Dioxide ($CO_2$) and from the lungs with Oxygen ($O_2$).

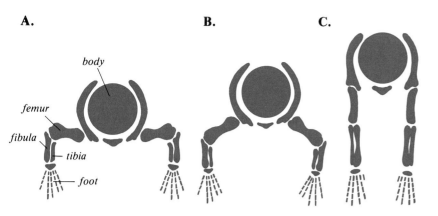

A.            B.            C.

*Limb posture and body stance of terrestrial, four-legged vertebrates.*
*A. Sprawling stance, typical of salamanders and most reptiles. In this stance the limbs extend from the sides of the body so that, while resting or moving slowly, the body is on or close to the ground.*
*B. Semi-erect stance, typical of crocodiles and some lizards. In this stance the body is raised clear of the ground when moving quickly but lowered to a sprawling stance when resting or walking slowly.*
*C. Fully-erect stance, typical of dinosaurs and mammals. In this stance, the limbs directly support the body and move in a vertical plane.*

Crocodilians, although cold-blooded, have a four-chambered heart; unlike birds and mammals, however, they have no insulating fur, feathers or layers of fat and cannot effectively control loss of body heat to the atmosphere.

Because the only living relatives of the dinosaurs—crocodilians and birds—have highly efficient four-chambered hearts, it follows that the dinosaurs did as well. It does not necessarily follow from this, however, that dinosaurs were warm-blooded. Judging from the scanty fossil evidence, at least some dinosaurs were covered with naked skin, pebbly in texture and devoid of scales, like the skin of turtles, with little, if any, obvious insulating characteristics.

The larger dinosaurs may have been able to maintain body heat and elevated activity levels by virtue of their sheer bulk alone—passive endothermism: The larger the animal, the smaller its skin area relative to its heat-generating body mass, and the slower it loses heat to the atmosphere. Some of the larger reptiles of today, such as the huge marine leatherback turtle (*Dermochelys coriacea*), which may weigh well over half a ton, and the larger pythons have a limited ability to raise their body temperature slightly above the temperature of their surroundings. This may have been true of the dinosaurs as well.

The body stances of dinosaurs definitely suggest an active life style. Dinosaurs had erect postures; they carried their bodies well off the ground on either two or four legs that were gathered under them and swung in a more or less mammalian fashion. By contrast, living reptiles appear awkward with their sprawling gait, elbows and knees akimbo, and legs splayed to the side.

Microscopic study of dinosaur bones shows a cellular structure that appears to be more mammalian than reptilian in character, also suggestive of a warm-blooded condition. Some physiologists, however, suggest that this may be related to growth processes common to all large, fast-growing vertebrates; it does not necessarily suggest an ability to regulate body heat.

Attempts have been made to equate activity levels of dinosaurs with their relative brain size, with limited success. Predatory dinosaurs, in general, had somewhat larger brain cavities than did herbivorous species. But all dinosaurs had essentially reptilian brains, and it is difficult to relate brain size to physiological levels, except in general terms, when dealing with extinct forms of life.

One ingenious argument is based upon the low number of carnivorous dinosaurs relative to the number of plant-eaters in any given dinosaur fauna, as reconstructed from their fossil remains. Warm-blooded animals, because they burn up energy at a faster rate, need more food than do cold-blooded animals of the same size. In communities of warm-blooded animals, therefore, there will be relatively fewer predators because each would require a larger share of the available food supply.

The number of carnivorous species has been estimated at a low three to fourteen percent of the total number of dinosaurs in various fossil assemblages—about the same as in modern mammalian (warm-blooded) faunas. Some scientists have challenged these figures and suggest that the larger dinosaurs may have required just as much food as warm-blooded animals of the same size merely by virtue of their great bulk. What is really needed is a live dinosaur or two!

Yet another conjecture proposes that, because primitive mammals, assumed to be fully warm-blooded, appeared as early in the fossil record as did primitive dinosaurs, dinosaurs could not possibly have been as successful as they were in becoming the dominant form of terrestrial life throughout the Mesozoic if they had not been warm-blooded as well. We can only surmise.

All lines of study, although indirect and open to challenge, suggest that dinosaurs led a more active life than do the reptiles of today; that their metabolic levels were correspondingly higher; and that they probably could regulate their internal temperature to a much greater extent. Dinosaurs were an extremely diverse group of reptiles, and it would be surprising if their physiological makeups were not varied as well. Taken as a whole, their anatomical structure would suggest that they were not as physiologically advanced as are modern birds and mammals. And whether they were able to function efficiently in other than tropical, or near tropical, environments remains conjectural.

Dinosaurs and the world they lived in are gone. We are left with only one clear observation: For whatever reason, they could not adapt.

# The Triassic Period

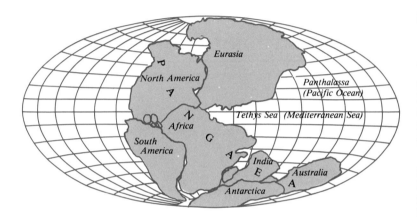

*In the early Triassic, all the earth's land surfaces were connected as one supercontinent called Pangaea. In the illustration, present-day continents of North America, Eurasia, South America, Africa, India, Antarctica and Australia are indicated. The Tethys Sea was the ancestral Mediterranean and Panthalassa, the ancestral Pacific Ocean. Adapted from "The Break-Up of Pangaea" by Robert S. Dietz and John C. Holden. Copyright © 1970 by Scientific American, Inc. All rights reserved.*

## Climate and Geography

The Triassic Period of 245 to 208 million years ago represents the earliest portion of the Mesozoic Era. The name *Triassic,* derived from the Latin word *trias,* refers to a series of three well-defined fossiliferous deposits from this period discovered in Germany.

A globe showing the distribution of land and sea at the beginning of the Triassic Period would look strikingly different from the world we know today. During the early Triassic, all of the earth's land masses were joined together into one great supercontinent Pangaea. The continental shelves of what are today known as North and South America were up against those of what is now Europe and Africa. Rifts which would later lead to the separation of today's continents were beginning to appear in the late Triassic. Land animals and plants, however, could still easily spread across the supercontinent. Triassic plant and animal fossils from deposits found on a variety of continents are thus more similar than are the living plants and animals of the various continents today.

The climate during the Triassic was generally mild, but there seem to have been periods of aridity which resulted in sizable deserts. Compared with the earlier Paleozoic Era and the Jurassic and Cretaceous Periods that were to follow, during the Triassic very little of the continental surface was under water. Seas, advancing north into Germany in the middle Triassic and retreating south again in the late Triassic, did, however, cover what is now the Alpine region of Europe.

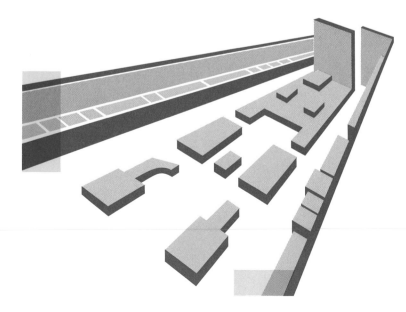

*Dinosaur Hall Triassic fossils (detailed floorplan on p. 113)*

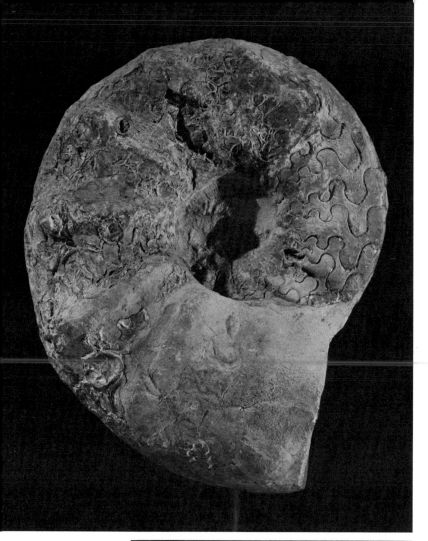

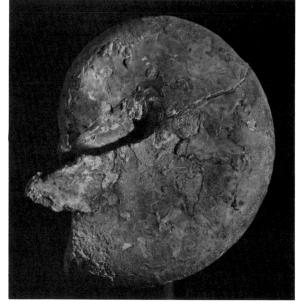

*Upper left:* Ceratites nodosus *(C.M. Invertebrate Fossil No. 29863), a Triassic ammonite. Although related to the present-day chambered nautilus, chambers of the ammonite differed from those of the nautilus. While the sutures between the nautilus' chambers are relatively straight, those between the ammonite's chambers were often irregular and connected to the external shell in a variety of ways. Some of the sutures and chambers of the fossilized* Ceratites nodosus *can be seen.* **Upper right:** Cladiscites tornatus *(C.M. Invertebrate Fossil No. 28002), another Triassic ammonite. Although ammonites originated in the middle Paleozoic, they reached their peak of development during the Mesozoic Era. By the end of the Triassic, ammonites exhibited various styles of external ornamentation including ribs and surface nodes.* **Lower left:** Monophyllites simonyi *(C.M. Invertebrate Fossil No. 28006), a large Triassic ammonite. Although now extinct, this squid-like animal is related to the chambered nautilus of today. Ammonites floated on the open seas but could move backward by squirting a jet of water through their tentacled mouth.*

*Right:* Encrinus lilliformis *(C.M. Invertebrate Fossil Nos. 27997 & 27998), a now-extinct marine echinoderm of the Triassic that lived attached to the sea bottom. The smaller specimen shows a sea lily with its branches opened while the larger specimen shows the branches closed. In life, these branches were covered with beating cilia that directed a stream of food-bearing water to the mouth.*

# Triassic Invertebrates, Reptiles and Amphibians

## Marine Fossils

Brachiopods, shelled invertebrates superficially resembling clams, suffered a marked decline—from which they never recovered—in numbers and varieties at the end of the Paleozoic Era. A few did survive until the end of the Triassic. These included *Athyris miles,* on exhibit in Dinosaur Hall.

Another group of invertebrate fossils on display are the ammonites, a type of cephalopod ("head-foot") that has tentacles around the mouth and can move backwards rapidly by squirting a jet of water forward. A typical ammonite was a squid-like animal that lived in a superficially snail-like shell and floated on the open sea. Although the ammonite resembled its present-day relative the chambered nautilus, studies indicate that an important difference between the two animals exists: While the partitions between the chambers in the nautilus are relatively straight, those in the ammonite were crumpled and connected to the walls of the external shell in a variety of patterns. Because of the variety and widespread distribution of ammonites in the past, paleontologists have used them extensively to determine the geologic age of rocks throughout the world.

The ammonites, like the brachiopods, suffered a severe setback at the close of the Paleozoic Era and nearly became extinct. They recovered, however, in the Triassic Period and evolved into many new types. These new ammonites were threatened with extinction at the close of the Triassic but, once again, managed to survive.

The majority of Triassic ammonites tended to have relatively simple sutures, the lines marking the junction of the chamber wall with the external wall of the shell. By the latter part of the Triassic, the ammonites displayed a considerable variety of external ornamentation such as ribs and nodes on the exterior surface of the shell. Three examples of large Triassic ammonites are exhibited: *Ceratites nodosus, Cladiscites tornatus,* and

*Monophyllites simonyi.* As can be seen, part of the outer shell layer of the fossilized *Ceratites* has broken away, exposing its sutures.

The carapace, or top shell, of the lobster-like *Pemphix sueri* is also displayed. Arthropods (joint-limbed animals such as crabs) had been in existence since the Precambrian Era. Throughout the early periods of the Paleozoic Era, the trilobites were the predominant arthropod bottom dwellers. By the end of the Paleozoic Era, however, the trilobites had disappeared, and other marine arthropods—the lobsters and their kin—replaced them.

The Triassic seas also contained echinoderms, including such modern examples as starfish, sea lilies (crinoids), sea cucumbers and sand dollars. One Triassic sea lily, *Encrinus lilliformis,* can be seen on exhibit. Remains of sea lilies are common fossils from the Paleozoic Era to the present. Modern echinoderms, including stemmed forms and the free-floating feather stars, first appear in the Triassic. They superceded an array of older lineages that died out at the end of the Paleozoic.

*Top:* Lariosaurus *sp. (C.M. Vertebrate Fossil No. 8946), a Triassic nothosaur. Like the present-day crocodile, members of this early marine reptile group were probably amphibious.* Lariosaurus *most likely ate fish and other forms of marine life. It probably retreated to the shore in order to rest and breed.* **Bottom:** Redfieldius gracilis *(C.M. Vertebrate Fossil No. 5301), a primitive bony fish from the late Triassic of Connecticut. These fish had thicker scales and a less symmetrical tail than modern bony fish.*

*Page 37:* Placodus *sp. lower jaw (C.M. Vertebrate Fossil No. 2776). These peculiar Triassic reptiles, called placodonts, had a turtle-like, bony armor and jaws and teeth modified for crushing the shells of molluscs.*

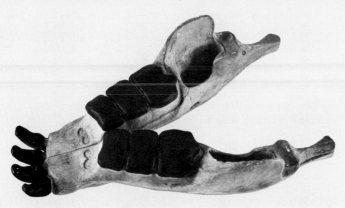

### The Reptiles Return to the Sea

During the Mesozoic Era, several lineages of reptiles became amphibious, and some became successful marine animals. Two different kinds are displayed in Dinosaur Hall. Both of these reptiles probably fed in the sea but crawled out on land to rest and breed. One of these reptiles on display, *Placodus,* vaguely resembled a fat lizard about 7 feet (2 m) long. Its feet were webbed, and the forefeet had long claws. Nodules of bones embedded under the skin gave some protection to the spine.

Although it resembled a lizard, the skull and teeth of *Placodus* were definitely not lizard-like. Teeth on the palate and on the margins of the jaws were flat, crushing plates. Those at the front of the mouth were widely spaced and projected forward. The jaw muscles were extremely powerful. *Placodus* almost certainly fed on snails and other hard-shelled molluscs. The claws and projecting teeth raked in the meal, and the flat teeth crushed the shells.

From *Placodus* or a closely related reptile evolved turtle-like placodonts in the middle and late Triassic. In them the nodules along the spine multiplied into a complete, flattened armor plate that covered the body. The front teeth were lost and replaced by a horny beak. All four legs became paddle-like which made the placodonts resemble sea turtles. Turtles, which also first appeared in the Triassic, are either vegetarians or carnivorous, but placodonts remained solely mollusc eaters.

The other reptile on display, *Lariosaurus,* also looked somewhat like a large lizard with a long neck. *Lariosaurus* had a long snout equipped with many slender, pointed teeth used for eating fish. The front feet were paddle-like, and the hind feet, webbed. The nearly complete *Lariosaurus* skeleton, on display from its belly side, exhibits clearly the protective sheath of belly ribs (gastralia) found in many other kinds of reptiles—including some dinosaurs.

*Lariosaurus*-like reptiles were the ancestors of the plesiosaurs which flourished in the Jurassic and Cretaceous seas. Some plesiosaurs had very large heads and short necks, while others had very long necks and small heads. All of the plesiosaurs had four legs that served as paddles, and all had relatively short tails.

### An Amphibian Disaster in the Western United States

By the late Triassic, the amphibians were no longer the dominant land vertebrates. Those that persisted were either small, relatively inconspicuous insect eaters or much larger species that had reverted to an entirely aquatic existence. With its huge head, flattened body, and feeble legs, *Metoposaurus* lurked in fresh water ponds where it probably fed on fish and invertebrates. One pond in what is now north-central New Mexico was home for at least several hundred metoposaurs. The pond gradually dried up, perhaps during a drought, and the giant amphibians crowded into what had been the deepest portion. There, piled on top of each other, they died. The decaying carcasses of the dead were partly dismembered by the struggles of those that still lived. Eventually the rains returned and washed clay and sand over the remains. More than fifty metoposaurs were thus preserved, including the two skulls, part of a third skull and some bone material on exhibit.

# Fishes and Tracks of Dinosaurs in the Eastern United States

What we now know as the Appalachian Mountains—along the east coast of North America, from Newfoundland to Florida—first formed during the Paleozoic Era. During the Triassic Period, these mountains gradually eroded away; and, during the late Triassic and early Jurassic, they were bordered by steadily sinking trough-like basins. One of these basins ran north-south through what is now New England, and another ran east-west across southeastern Pennsylvania. Deposits containing fossils from the Triassic Period left in these basins are known as the Newark Group. In central Connecticut, some of the sedimentary rock from the Newark Group contains abundant remains of Triassic land plants and fresh water fish. The sandstone of the Connecticut Valley is also famous for the tracks of dinosaurs.

Two fish from the Newark Group are displayed in Dinosaur Hall. *Redfieldius gracilis* was a member of a group of primitive, bony fish prominent in the Paleozoic Era. In comparison to earlier members of the group, *Redfieldius* had a shorter, more mobile mouth and a more symmetrical tail. As in most early bony fish, the scales were thick and shiny because of a layer of enamel, the same substance which forms the outer layer of teeth. Most modern bony fish have lost this enamel layer and, instead, have thin, flexible scales. Before the end of the Cretaceous Period, this group of early bony fish declined and became extinct.

The second fish from the Newark Group on display, *Semionotus micropterus,* is a member of a group of more-advanced bony fish prominent throughout the Mesozoic Era. This more-advanced group, common in the Triassic and early Jurassic Periods, is also extinct, except for the bowfin and the gars. In comparison to the earlier group of which *Redfieldius* was a member, the more-advanced bony fish were better adapted in the mobility of mouth and tail.

Late Triassic amphibians, reptiles, and fish are also known from bones and teeth found at sites in southeastern Pennsylvania and adjacent areas of New Jersey. None of these southeastern Pennsylvania fossils are exhibited here, but life-size restorations of many Triassic vertebrates are displayed at the William Penn Memorial Museum in Harrisburg. Among these restorations are the flattened amphibian *Metoposaurus,* which was similar to Carnegie Museum's specimens from New Mexico. The coelacanth fish *Diplurus,* which is closely related to the ancestors of amphibians, is also displayed in Harrisburg.

Two other reptiles were also known to have inhabited the Pennsylvania landscape. *Hypsognathus* and *Sophodrosaurus,* with their solidly roofed skulls, looked like large, fat lizards. The details of the head structure of *Sophodrosaurus* are unknown, but paleontologists agree that *Hypsognathus* had four horns projecting from each side of its head, vaguely recalling a horned lizard

of today. Both were among the last survivors of their lineages.

*Stegomus,* an armored thecodont about 59 inches (1.5 m) long, was also included in the late Triassic animal life in Pennsylvania. This animal was distantly related to the ancestors of the dinosaurs, but the only actual remains of a dinosaur known thus far from Pennsylvania are the teeth of *Thecodontosaurus,* a plant-eater.

In the Triassic forests of Pennsylvania, the lizard *Icarosaurus* soared from branch to branch much the same as the modern lizard, the "flying dragon" of the Orient, does today. A membrane stretching between its enormously elongated ribs allowed *Icarosaurus* to glide.

The largest reptile known from the Newark Group is *Rutiodon,* which looked like a crocodile except that its nostrils were on top of a hump just in front of its eyes. Partial remains of one *Rutiodon* specimen from Pennsylvania indicate that it was approximately 15 or 16 feet (4.7 m) long.

Footprints of primitive dinosaurs and other reptiles have been discovered in late Triassic rock of Pennsylvania and New Jersey. At least two localities in southeastern Pennsylvania are among those where early reptiles left permanent records of their footsteps. One example of dinosaur tracks found in Adams County, near York Springs, Pennsylvania, attributed to *Anchisauripus,* is in Carnegie Museum of Natural History's collection. Although dinosaurs from the Triassic were generally bipedal, these tracks indicate that this was a four-footed dinosaur.

One early fossil collector, Edward B. Hitchcock, came across many tracks of two-footed Triassic dinosaurs. In 1835, Hitchcock began to collect and study fossil tracks found in a portion of the Newark Group located in Connecticut. Mistakenly, Hitchcock believed the three-toed tracks of early dinosaurs were made by flocks of gigantic, ostrich-like birds. His error is forgiven, however, since dinosaurs were not named until 1842, and the knowledge that many of them ran about on bird-like hind feet was not substantiated until the late 1850s.

*Top:* Semionotus micropterus *(C.M. Vertebrate Fossil No. 5287), a late Triassic relative of the modern gars and bowfin. These fish had a mobile mouth and tail, but not to the extent seen in most modern bony fish.* *Middle: Restoration of* Metoposaurus, *a large amphibian from the Triassic of southeastern Pennsylvania. Courtesy of the Pennsylvania Historical and Museum Commission—William Penn Memorial Museum.* *Bottom: Restoration of* Rutiodon, *a 15- or 16-foot long phytosaur from the Triassic of Pennsylvania. To facilitate breathing while partially immersed in water, the nostrils of this semi-aquatic reptile were just in front of the eyes, on a hump near the top of the skull. Courtesy of the Pennsylvania Historical and Museum Commission—William Penn Memorial Museum.*

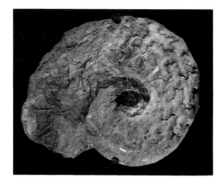

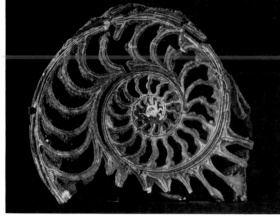

*Top: Jurassic ammonite (C.M. Invertebrate Fossil No. 33645). Although close to extinction at the beginning of the Jurassic, ammonites recovered and developed into a variety of forms throughout the period. In some areas, ammonites were so prevalent that fossil beds are composed entirely of their shells. **Middle:** Jurassic ammonite (C.M. Invertebrate Fossil No. 33646). The chambers can be seen in this ammonite which has been cut in half. The living animal originally occupied the central chamber. As the animal grew, it occupied successively larger quarters. The last and largest chamber of the ammonite contained most of the soft-bodied parts of the animal. Ammonites controlled bouyancy by varying the pressure in their abandoned, gas-filled chambers. **Bottom:** Jurassic rock containing the fossilized remains of · marine animals (C.M. Invertebrate Fossil No. 29803). Found in Wyoming, this rock was formed by sediments deposited in the shallow Sundance Sea that covered parts of the western United States. The remains of numerous marine organisms including ammonites and small clam shells can be seen in the rock.*

# The Jurassic Period

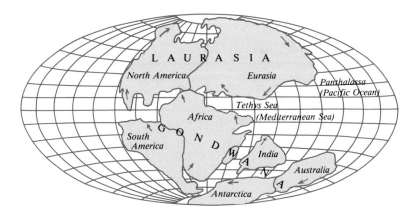

*By the early Jurassic, the northern group of continents, known as Laurasia, had separated from the southern group, known as Gondwana. Laurasia included the present-day continents of North America and Eurasia, while Gondwana included the present-day South America, Africa, India, Antarctica and Australia. The Tethys Sea was the ancestral Mediterranean and Panthalassa was the ancestral Pacific Ocean. The arrows in the illustration indicate the direction in which the continents were drifting. Adapted from "The Break-Up of Pangaea" by Robert S. Dietz and John C. Holden. Copyright © 1970 by Scientific American, Inc. All rights reserved.*

## Climate and Geography

During the Jurassic Period present-day continents were still partially joined together as one giant land mass. A northern portion, composed of what is now North America, Greenland, and northern and central Eurasia, however, had begun to rift and drift away from the southern portion. The similarity in some land animals between the northern and southern portions suggests that the two portions were still connected, perhaps through Spain and northern Africa.

Seas covered more of the land during the 69 million years of the Jurassic than in the Triassic. As a result, the climate was milder. Four times during the Jurassic Period a shallow sea, named Sundance Sea by geologists, spread south from the present-day Arctic Circle to what is now North America, covering the region where the Rocky Mountains rise today. Another sea, which never connected with the Sundance Sea, covered the Gulf Coast and parts of Mexico during the Jurassic. A third sea, separated from the Sundance Sea by a narrow strip of land, extended over the Pacific Northwest as far south as northern California.

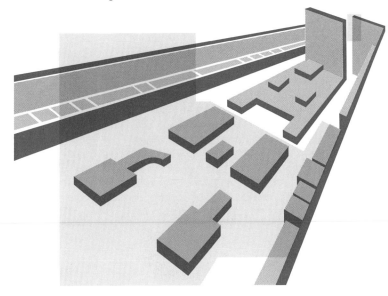

*Dinosaur Hall Jurassic fossils (detailed floorplan on p. 113)*

Near the end of the Jurassic, the Sundance Sea withdrew to the north, leaving a vast basin that covered Montana, Wyoming, Colorado, and portions of adjacent states. During this time the rocks lying to the west of this area—in Utah, Nevada, Idaho, and on into California and Oregon—were being crushed, folded, and uplifted. Periods of volcanic activity accompanied the initial uplift of the resulting Sierra Nevada Mountain Range in present-day California and the Great Basin ranges in present-day Nevada. Rivers and streams carried sediments from higher ground located in the West, Southwest, and Northeast into basin regions. These sediments are the deposits that became the Morrison Formation, famous for the dinosaur fossils it contains.

North America east of the Sundance Sea was mostly above sea level. Here, there occurred little deposition in which dinosaurs and other animals could be preserved. Thus, although dinosaurs almost certainly lived in Pennsylvania and other northeastern states in the Jurassic, no record of their existence remains.

Seas also covered much of Europe during the Jurassic Period, so called because deposits from this period occur in the Jura Mountains of northern Switzerland and southern Germany. A great ocean trench occupied the area where today the Alps stand; this trench stretched eastward to the site of the Himalayas.

*Top:* Pachycormis ecocinus (C.M. Vertebrate Fossil No. 5243), a large, predaceous bony fish from the early Jurassic Holzmaden deposits of West Germany. This powerful swimmer, with a large head and toothed jaws, belongs to the group of bony fish that includes the modern gars and bowfin. *Bottom:* Stenopterygius sp. (C.M. Vertebrate Fossil No. 6003), a Jurassic ichthyosaur. This group of air-breathing reptiles first appeared during the Triassic Period. Stenopterygius bore its young alive while in the water.

# Holzmaden Fossils from the Early Jurassic

Holzmaden in the southern part of West Germany is one area where grayish-black, fine-grained limestone was deposited during the early Jurassic. The limestone quarries located there are noted for the superbly preserved remains of marine life they contain. A fish, a fish-like reptile, a marine crocodile, and a flying reptile from the Holzmaden deposits are on exhibit in Dinosaur Hall.

*Pachycormis* was a Jurassic fish whose fossilized remains were found in the Holzmaden deposits. This fish had a narrow yet deep body with thick, shiny scales. Its pointed snout was set with teeth, and its body ended with a powerful, tuna-like tail. Undoubtedly, *Pachycormis* preyed on other fish and marine animals. Today, the bowfin is its closest living relative. *Pachycormis esocinus* has been particularly well preserved. Under close examination, evidence of its body scales and the fine teeth which lined its snout can be seen.

*Stenopterygius* is another marine fossil from the Holzmaden deposits. In this exquisitely preserved fossil the body is clearly outlined. Its bony flippers, two-lobed tail, vertebral column, neural spine, eye sockets, and teeth are distinguishable. Despite its fins and streamlined body, *Stenopterygius* was actually an air-breathing reptile. Such fish-like reptiles are known as ichthyosaurs ("fish-lizard"). First found in marine deposits from the Triassic, ichthyosaurs typically had a long, toothed beak, enormous eyes, and flipper-like limbs. In complete, articulated ichthyosaur skeletons such as the one in Dinosaur Hall, the tail bones turn abruptly down near the end of the tail. When paleontologists first discovered ichthyosaurs, they assumed the tail was broken and proceeded to straighten it out during the restoration of the skeleton. Later, when ichthyosaurs were discovered in the Holzmaden deposits, the outline of the entire body was preserved. Paleontologists then realized that the ichthyosaurs had a fish-like tail and a dorsal fin.

Ichthyosaurs probably had habits similar to porpoises of today. They were fish eaters and incapable of walking on land. Some Holzmaden ichthyosaur skeletons with the young still inside the mother indicate that, unlike most reptiles that lay their eggs on land, ichthyosaurs bore their young alive and in the water. In one known fossil, a baby ichthyosaur is in the place where the birth canal would have been. Apparently, the mother either died while she was giving birth or she delivered the baby ichthyosaur just after she died.

The marine crocodile from the Holzmaden deposits on exhibit is *Steneosaurus*. This marine animal was a crocodilian, a member of the sole group of archosaurs that survived the mass extinction of reptiles at the end of the Cretaceous Period.

Like other early crocodilians, *Steneosaurus* had a well-developed armor plating under its skin. Its habits and general appearance resembled the gavial, a present-day crocodilian inhabiting the river systems of India and Pakistan. Although *Steneosaurus* could still walk easily on the shore, some of its descendants or close relatives in the late Jurassic and early Cretaceous evolved paddle-like legs and a tail fin. Its long, slender nose and sharp teeth show that *Steneosaurus* was a fish eater. As in the fish *Pachycormis* and the ichthyosaur *Steneopterygius,* the shape of *Steneosaurus'* snout minimized water resistance. This allowed *Steneosaurus* to swing its head from side to side and seize fish with great speed.

Many of *Steneosaurus'* features can be noted in the fossilized example on exhibit in Dinosaur Hall. Particularly evident are the crocodilian's armored plates which were anchored in place by pits under the skin.

Holzmaden has yielded remains of another particularly intriguing group of archosaurs, the pterosaurs. Pterosaurs had four fingers on each hand. The first three, equivalents of our thumb, index, and middle fingers, respectively, were like those of typical reptiles and bore claws. The fourth finger was extremely elongated and was used to support a membrane of skin that attached to the body to create a long wing. The pterosaurs' hind legs were slender and weak.

Superficially, pterosaurs looked like bats, but in some respects they were more like birds. Their thin-walled limb bones were hollow and filled with air; this greatly reduced their weight. The eyes of the pterosaur were large, and the olfactory bulbs of the brain were small; pterosaurs probably had excellent eyesight but a poor sense of smell. Also as in birds, the brain's cerebral hemispheres, where flight control is found, were greatly enlarged, and their necks were relatively

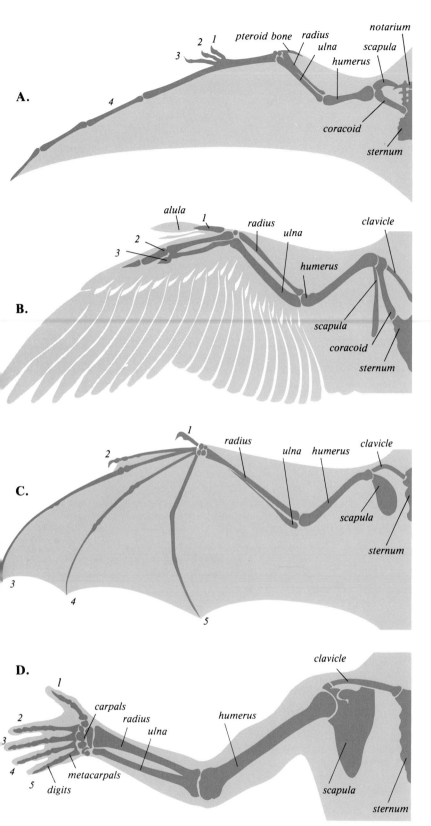

**A.**

2 1
3
pteroid bone    radius
ulna
4    humerus    scapula    notarium
coracoid
sternum

**B.**

alula    1
2    radius
3    ulna    clavicle
humerus
scapula
coracoid
sternum

**C.**

1    radius
2    ulna    humerus    clavicle
3    scapula
4    sternum
5

**D.**

1    clavicle
2    carpals
3    radius
ulna    humerus
4    metacarpals    scapula
5    digits    sternum

*A comparison of wings and the human forelimb. The wing of a pterosaur, a bird and a bat and the forelimb of a human are all built of the same bones. Each represents an evolutionary variation on the forelimb of a fully terrestrial animal and each evolved independently during the Mesozoic and Cenozoic Eras.*
*A. Pterosaur wing. The wing is supported by a greatly elongated fourth finger.*
*B. Bird wing. In the bird, the arm bones and the second finger support the wing.*
*C. Bat wing. This wing is supported by the arm bones and all fingers except the first.*
*D. Human forelimb. The position of the humerus, radius and ulna correspond with that found in the pterosaur, bird and bat.*

***Below:*** *Campylognathoides sp. (C.M. Vertebrate Fossil No. 11424), a long-tailed pterosaur of the early Jurassic. This crow-sized pterosaur specimen is the best preserved of those found in Holzmaden deposits and the only* Campylognathoides *specimen in the United States.*

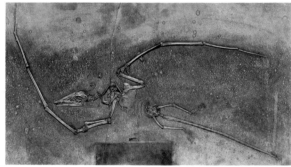

long and flexible. Unlike modern birds, however, earlier pterosaurs had slender snouts armed with sharp teeth. Some pterosaurs were further distinguished from birds by the presence of a long tail.

Compared to those of birds and bats, pterosaur wings were extremely fragile. If birds lose flight feathers, they still can fly. Tears to bats' wings are minimized by the placement of four of their five fingers within the wing membrane; the placement of the four fingers provides support and makes the wing more flexible. Each of the pterosaurs' wings, on the other hand, were supported merely by a single finger running along the wing's outer edge. An injury or tear could make a wing non-functional and, thus, permanently ground the pterosaur.

The earliest known pterosaurs occur in the late Triassic. They probably evolved from the thecodonts, which were also the ancestors of crocodiles, ornithischians, saurischians (and their descendants, birds). The pterosaurs have no living descendants.

Pterosaurs are classified into two groups. The earliest known pterosaurs and all early Jurassic ones are categorized as long-tailed pterosaurs. This group typically had short necks and short faces. Although their wrists were also relatively short, their fourth-finger—which supported the wing membrane—was long. The last of the long-tailed pterosaurs occurred in the late Jurassic Period.

The other group was the short-tailed pterosaurs. These appeared during the late Jurassic and survived until the close of the Mesozoic Era. Along with their short-tails, these pterosaurs had long faces, long necks, and wrists which were long in comparison to their fourth fingers.

The long-tailed pterosaur *Campylognathoides* in Dinosaur Hall was discovered in 1897 by Bernard Hauff, a noted preparator of fossils. This crow-sized pterosaur is one of the most important specimens in the Museum's collection of Holzmaden fossils. Although the skull was missing at the time Hauff found the skeleton, a year later it was discovered in the same level at the Holzmaden quarry yet about 15 feet (several meters) away. A slight current had apparently carried the head away from the decaying carcass before it was covered with mud and preserved.

While preparing the pterosaur fossil, Hauff placed the head back in its proper position. Of the five specimens of *Campylognathoides* known worldwide, this specimen is the best preserved and the only one in America.

Except for the first five or six vertebrae, *Campylognathoides'* tail bones were surrounded by thin, bony rods that made the long tail stiff and almost immovable. Paleontologists agree that *Rhamphorhynchus,* another long-tailed pterosaur on display in Dinosaur Hall, had a vertical membrane at the end of its tail that helped in steering by serving as a rudder or balancing structure. *Campylognathoides* possibly sported a similar structure that aided in flight at the end of its tail.

# Middle Jurassic Invertebrates

In the middle of the Jurassic, the seas covering much of Europe began to recede. For the first time in the earth's history, coral reefs formed by scleractinian corals whose shape is based on a basic hexagonal structure, became widespread in shallow waters. Although known as early as the late Paleozoic, these corals did not become predominant until the middle or late Jurassic.

One of the exhibit cases in Dinosaur Hall displays two kinds of scleractinian corals along with other kinds of invertebrates that lived on the reefs. The tubular-shaped *Calamophyllia stokesi* and squat-shaped *Thecosmilia annularis* can be seen in the case along with the sponge *Hyalotragos pezizoides,* the molluscs *Antiquilima antiquata* and *Alectryonia marshii,* and the sea urchin *Plegiocidaris coronata.*

Jurassic ammonites are also displayed in Dinosaur Hall. Four large, well-preserved ammonites from Solnhofen and other European deposits can be seen in one exhibit case. Two even larger ammonites are exhibited on the wall above this case.

As mentioned earlier, ammonites had been threatened with extinction at the close of the Triassic. Few, however, managed to survive and evolved into a new array of forms during the Jurassic.

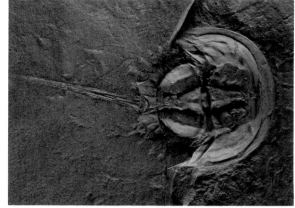

**Top left:** Eryon *sp. (C.M. Invertebrate Fossil No. 33072), a marine arthropod from the late Jurassic Solnhofen deposits. Its distant living relative is the spiny lobster.* **Top right:** Mesolimulus walchi *(C.M. Invertebrate Fossil No. 28513), a horseshoe crab from the late Jurassic Solnhofen deposits.* **Bottom left:** Phylloceras heterophyllus *(C.M. Invertebrate Fossil No. 1195), an early Jurassic ammonite found near Salzburg, Austria. Although nothing remains of the original shell, sediment created a natural mold of the ammonite's shape. The fern-like pattern on the surface of the fossil are sutures.* **Bottom right:** Cenoceras *sp. (C.M. Invertebrate Fossil No. 25572), a nautiloid found in Jurassic deposits of England. The polished, external surface clearly shows the simple sutures which distinguish the nautiloids from ammonites.*

In addition to ammonites, other cephalopods are exhibited in Dinosaur Hall. These include coleoids such as *Acanthoteuthis speciosa, Plesioteuthis prisca, Belemnites,* and *Coccoteuthis hastiformis.* In the first two the tentacles and an outline of the head are obvious. Usually the pens—straight, internal shells that contained successively larger, walled-off living chambers—are all that remain of such cephalopods. In the cephalopods on exhibit, the pens have largely been recrystallized.

# Solnhofen and the Coral Reefs of the Late Jurassic

During the late Jurassic, a series of shallow, subtropical lagoons extended across Europe from Spain, through France, and into southern Germany. The pure, fine-grained limestones that were laid down in these lagoons have preserved a remarkable record of late Jurassic animal life. The best known deposits from this time period are the quarries in the vicinity of Solnhofen, in southern Germany. Quarried since Roman times for building stone and lithography, the Solnhofen limestone has yielded more than 600 species of fossil animals. It has, in some cases, preserved the impressions of soft body parts that are usually lost in the fossilization process.

These Solnhofen deposits are well known for fossil insects. Although Carnegie Museum of Natural History possesses such fossils, none are currently on display. Most animals found in the Solnhofen deposits were free swimming and floating marine forms, but reptiles and various kinds of flying creatures (including insects, pterosaurs, and the earliest known birds) were also uncovered. A few of the finest from the Bayet Collection are displayed.

One of the most common of the Solnhofen fossils is the little crinoid *Saccocoma.* Like today's feather stars, *Saccocoma* floated freely, moving by waving its arms. Distinctive, wing-like expansions on the bases of the arms may have helped it to swim more efficiently. This little crinoid can be seen in one of Dinosaur Hall's exhibit cases along with *"Antedon" formosus,* another free-floating feather star.

Several marine arthropods from the Solnhofen deposits are also on display. These include the relatives of the spiny lobster: *Eryon* sp., *Palinurina longipes,* and *Phalangites priscus.* The first two are well preserved with the body outline and appendages clearly indicated. The third specimen noted above may be the larval form of *Palinurina longipes.* A relative of the living lobster, *Eryma leptodactylus,* is also displayed. Other marine arthropods shown are the horseshoe crab *Mesolimulus walchi* and the prawns (shrimps) *Aeger tipularius* and *Antrimpos speciosus.*

Many kinds of fish swam in the lagoons that extended over the Solnhofen area during the Jurassic. Among these were sharks and rays similar to their counterparts today. The little shark *Cestracion,* closely related to the living Port Jackson shark of the Pacific Ocean, is exhibited in Dinosaur Hall. Like the Port Jackson shark, *Cestracion* ate molluscs; it also had sharp fangs in the front of its mouth and low, rounded teeth in the rear for crushing shells. A stout spine supported each of the two dorsal fins. Usually, fin spines and isolated teeth are all that remain of fossil sharks and their kin because their skeletons are made entirely of cartilage instead of bone. Both the vertebral column and fin spines, however, can easily be distinguished in *Cestracion zittelli.*

Another Solnhofen specimen, the angel shark *Squatina,* appeared during the Jurassic and still lives today. This shark superficially resembles a skate or ray, with a flattened body and eyes on top of the head. However, the large pectoral fins evident in *Squatina alifera* are not attached to the body and the gills are at the sides of the body instead of underneath.

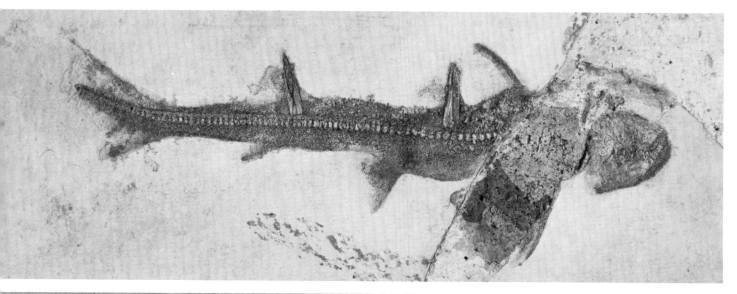

*Top:* Cestracion zitteli *(C.M. Vertebrate Fossil No. 4423), a small shark from the late Jurassic Solnhofen deposits. Like its close relative, the modern Port Jackson shark found in the Pacific Ocean,* Cestracion *had low, rounded teeth for crushing mollusc shells.* **Middle:** Aeger tipularius *(C.M. Invertebrate Fossil No. 33123), a late Jurassic shrimp from the Solnhofen deposits.* **Bottom:** Squatina alifera *(C.M. Vertebrate Fossil No. 5397), a fossil angel shark from the late Jurassic deposits of Eichstätt, Bavaria. This shark, with a flattened body and expanded pectoral fins, was a sea-bottom dweller. It is closely related to living angel sharks.*

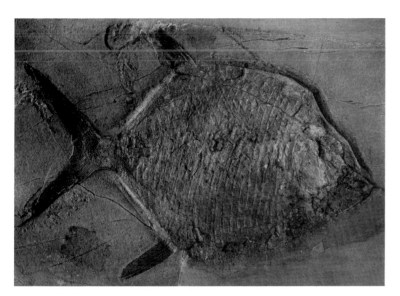

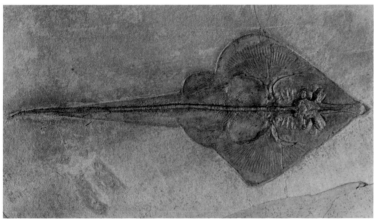

*Top:* Gyrodus circularis *(C.M. Vertebrate Fossil No. 4407), a late Jurassic pycnodont from the Solnhofen deposits. These fish, with deep, flat, circular bodies, lived among coral reefs. They had short, beak-shaped jaws and pebble-like teeth for feeding on coral.* **Middle:** Belemnobatis sismondae *(C.M. Vertebrate Fossil No. 4408) from the late Jurassic Solnhofen deposits. This bottom-dweller had a flattened body and expanded front fins. It fed on molluscs and other invertebrates.* Belemnobatis *resembles its closest living relative, the banjo fish.* **Bottom:** *Three bony fish from the late Jurassic Solnhofen deposits.* Thrissops formosus *(C.M. Vertebrate Fossil No. 4030) (top left), a predaceous fish that descended from* Leptolepis *and an ancestor of the living tarpon.* Leptolepis dubia *(C.M. Vertebrate Fossil No. 4692) (top right), an ancestral herring that swam in large schools in the Solnhofen sea.* Megalurus lepidotus *(C.M. Vertebrate Fossil No. 4732) (bottom), was a marine predator that resembled the living fresh water bowfin.*

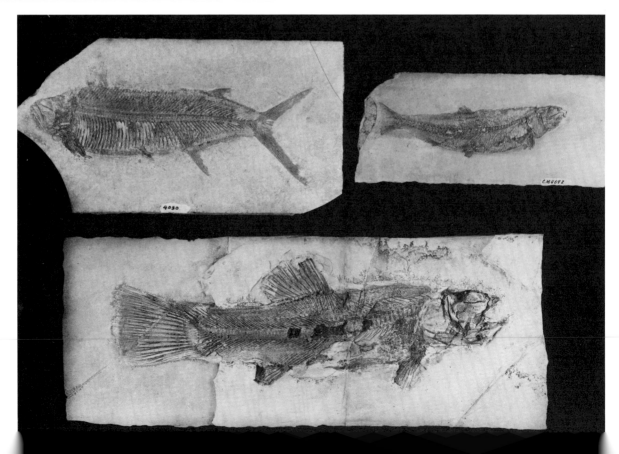

*Top:* Belonostomus *sp. (C.M. Vertebrate Fossil No. 4776). Superficially similar to the living garpike, this fish had a toothless, needle-like snout.* **Middle:** *A long-bodied predaceous fish from the Solnhofen deposits.* Sauropsis *sp. (C.M. Vertebrate Fossil No. 4761), a close relative of the early Jurassic* Pachycormis. **Bottom:** Plesiochelys etalloni *(C.M. Vertebrate Fossil No. 3410), a late Jurassic turtle from the Solnhofen deposits. Unlike the modern turtles,* Plesiochelys *probably could not retract its neck, feet and tail into the shell.*

*Belemnobatis,* now extinct, is in the same family as the living banjo fish. Like the angel shark, it was a bottom dweller and probably ate molluscs and other invertebrates by first crushing them with its distinctive battery of flat teeth. This fish's internal structure is clearly evident in *Belmnobatis sismondae,* the Solnhofen fossil on exhibit.

The holostean ray-finned fish, prominent during the Mesozoic, were very diverse and dominant in number of species. One member of this group, the heavy-bodied *Lepidotus,* was a widely distributed fish whose existence spanned that of the dinosaurs—from the late Triassic to the late Cretaceous. Like its only living relative, the garpike, *Lepidotus* had a short mouth with peg-like teeth that probably crushed hard-shelled or hard-bodied invertebrates. One of its prominent features—thick, shiny scales—is easily distinguishable in *Lepidotus ovatus,* the Solnhofen specimen on exhibit.

*Megalurus,* another fish discovered in the Solnhofen deposits, was similar in appearance to the living bowfin, a powerful predator. It had an elongated body and thin scales. One major difference distinguishes the bowfin from *Megalurus:* Bowfins live in fresh water whereas *Megalurus* was a marine fish.

Just as today, Jurassic fish with deep, narrow, almost circular bodies swam through the tropical coral reefs. These colorful fish, called pycnodonts, may have been ecologically similar and as brightly colored as the modern varieties, but the connections stop there. *Gyrodus* and other Jurassic pycnodonts had short, beak-shaped jaws equipped with pebble-like teeth that allowed them to nibble on corals, clearly shown by *Gyrodus circularis.*

Two long-bodied predators are also displayed. *Sauropsis* was closely related to *Pachycormis,* an early Jurassic fish previously mentioned. Its head and body scales are clearly indicated in the Solnhofen specimen. The second of the long-bodied predators on display, *Belonostomus,* has no close living relatives but looked like the garpike of today. It had a sharp, toothless, needle-like snout.

The most abundant fish in the Solnhofen sea was *Leptolepis,* an ancestral herring that swam in schools and was sometimes stranded on the mud flats when the tide receded. This fish, feeding as it swam through clouds of plankton, is the earliest known teleost, precursors of the modern ray-finned fish. The thin, bony scales of a *Leptolepis*-like fish are known, in fact, as far back as the late Triassic. Two small specimens of *Leptolepis sprattiformis* and the somewhat larger *Leptolepis dubia* are on view in Dinosaur Hall.

Along with all of the free swimming and floating marine forms previously mentioned, reptiles have also been discovered in the Solnhofen deposits. Turtles, one of the oldest surviving groups of reptiles, were among these.

Except for the earliest known turtles in the Triassic, turtles have, instead of teeth, a horny beak with cutting edges that act as shears to slice up food. Most Mesozoic turtles, including the early marine form *Plesiochelys,* probably could not withdraw their heads, feet, and tails into their shells. Although the weight of the shell in *Plesiochelys* was reduced by holes for increased ease of movement, these holes were not as large as they became in later sea turtles.

This trend toward reduction of the shell in aquatic turtles can be explained by the fact that the specific gravity of the shell is greater than that of flesh; with less shell and more exposed flesh, the turtle could swim more easily. Later sea turtles also developed paddle-like feet, but the turtles of the Mesozoic Era still had clawed feet such as those of an ordinary pond turtle and thus could easily scramble around on shore. These typical clawed feet are shown in the Solnhofen fossil of *Plesiochelys* on exhibit.

Another type of animal discovered in the Solnhofen deposits are pterosaurs. Unlike the early Jurassic Holzmaden *Campylognathoides* previously mentioned, the late Jurassic Solnhofen "winged reptile" shows the imprints of both the wing membranes and the membrane at the end of the tail.

When the first pterosaur was discovered in 1784, naturalists of the day could not decide if it were a mammal, bird, or reptile. Some thought its enormously elongated wing fingers were long, penguin-like flippers, and that the animal must have swam in the sea. In 1802 the French anatomist Baron Georges Cuvier compared the

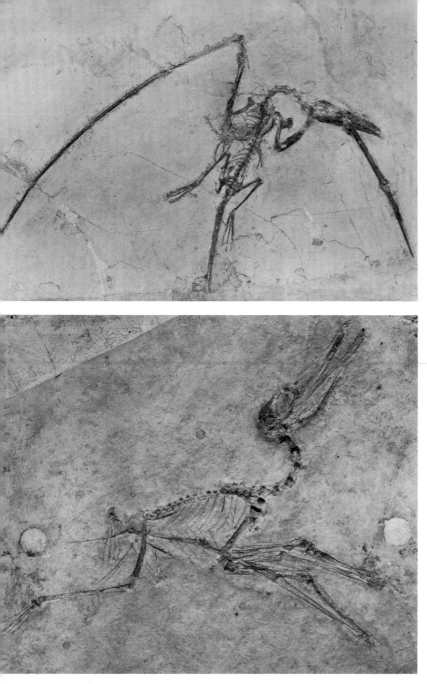

*Top:* Rhamphorynchus munsteri *(C.M. Vertebrate Fossil No. 11427), a long-tailed pterosaur of the late Jurassic. Found in Solnhofen deposits, this beautifully preserved specimen had a 42" wing span. The rear portion of its long jaws was lined with sharply pointed teeth. Paleontologists surmise that* Rhamphorynchus *glided over water and dived after small fish.* **Middle:** Pterodactylus elegans *(C.M. Vertebrate Fossil No. 11425), a short-tailed pterosaur of the late Jurassic. Found in Solnhofen deposits, this individual probably died and dried out on a beach or tidal flat. As its muscles dried, they contracted, curving the neck back and folding the wings.* **Bottom:** Pterodactylus sp. *(C.M. Vertebrate Fossil No. 11426), a short-tailed pterosaur of the late Jurassic. This robin-sized specimen from the Solnhofen deposits had a short, stubby tail. Its long, pointed jaws were lined with delicate teeth. Many have speculated as to how or if pterosaurs walked. Some paleontologists suggest that they walked bipedally, like birds. Other envision them walking on all four limbs, with the long wing fingers folded up out of the way.*

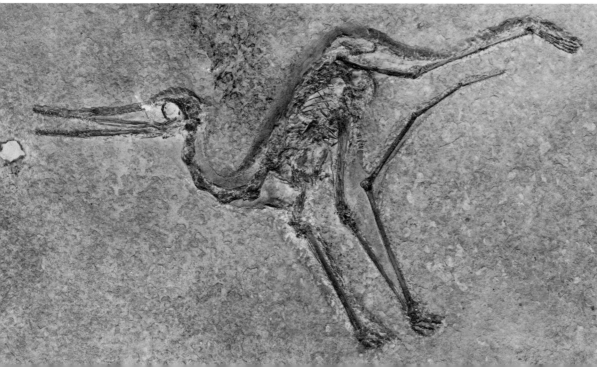

fossil carefully with skeletons of modern animals and pronounced it a flying reptile, unlike anything in existence in the modern world. Not until eight years later was Cuvier's deduction that the long finger supported a wing membrane proven correct.

O.C. Marsh, known also for his interest in dinosaurs, described a long-tailed Solnhofen pterosaur that had obvious wing membranes. The specimen also had a diamond-shaped flap at the end of its tail that may have served as a kind of rudder. When the Baron de Bayet purchased the *Rhamphorynchus munsteri,* displayed here, pterosaur skeletons with imprints of the membranes were still great rarities. Since that time, several others have been discovered.

*Rhamphorhynchus* had a short body, approximately a yard in length (91 cm). Because of its long beak with curious, sharply pointed teeth that slanted forward, most paleontologists assume *Rhamphorhynchus* fed on fish. They also surmise that the pterosaurs flew over and then dived after small fish, much as do modern marine birds.

By the late Jurassic, short-tailed pterosaurs had also appeared. Two robin-sizes specimens—*Pterodactylus elegans* and *Pterodactylus* sp.—are displayed. *Pterodactylus* was characterized by slender, delicate teeth restricted to the front of the jaws and a short, stubby tail. In the Cretaceous, the trend toward loss of teeth continued so that some pterosaurs became entirely toothless.

The position of the *Pterodactylus* specimens on display in Dinosaur Hall is typical of that of many pterosaurs found in the Solnhofen deposits. The animals probably died and dried out on a beach or tidal flat. As the muscles dried, they contracted, curving the neck back and folding the wings. Later the carcasses washed back into the sea and were buried on the bottom.

Paleontologists have long speculated that pterosaurs must have had a high level of metabolism to meet the energy requirements of flight; they must have been endotherms (warm-blooded). If so, they probably had some kind of external insulation to prevent excessive loss of heat. Although several pterosaurs with impressions of wing membranes have been recovered from the Solnhofen deposits, no feathers are present.

At least one early researcher believed he could see hair follicles on the wing membranes of one specimen, but others doubted him. Then, in 1971 a Russian paleontologist described a new pterosaur from late Jurassic lake deposits at Karatay in Kazakhstan. Its body was covered with thick, curly "hair." This find suggests that perhaps the bodies, if not the wing membranes, of other pterosaurs were also furry.

Students of the pterosaurs have often wondered how—and if—pterosaurs walked. Traditionally, pterosaurs are reconstructed with the hind legs attched to the wing membranes. With such an arrangement, they would have had great difficulty getting around on the ground. In a study completed in 1979, one paleontologist decided that the wing membranes actually were attached to the body in front of the hind legs and that pterosaurs walked bipedally, like birds. Other paleontologists envision them walking on all four feet, with the long wing fingers folded up out of the way. Perhaps pterosaurs even clambered around in trees and on cliffs, clinging with their hind feet and the clawed wing fingers. Through the lack of living evidence, the actual physical features of the pterosaur may never be known.

Two important species from Solnhofen not in Carnegie Museum of Natural History's collection should be mentioned. The first is *Archaeopteryx,* the earliest known bird. About the size of a pigeon, *Archaeopteryx* had a long tail with feathers along both sides. The forefeet had three fingers with well-developed claws, and its mouth was lined with small, sharp teeth. The hind legs and feet were like those of early dinosaurs and modern birds.

The development of the sternum (breast bone) and other skeletal characteristics show that *Archaeopteryx* was a poor flier. One paleontologist believes it ran on the ground after small animals it scooped up with the help of its long wing feathers and then seized with the claws of the forefeet.

The area where the Solnhofen deposits were found was also the home of *Compsognathus,* the rooster-size dinosaur that, until recently, was the smallest dinosaur known.

*Canyon at Dinosaur National Monument. This spectac-
ular canyon was cut through the Uinta Mountains by
the Green River. The mountain rocks, tipped up at a
67° angle, were once a sandbar where the carcasses of
Jurassic dinosaurs become lodged. Over millions of
years, sediment piled up on top of the dinosaurs and
became rock. The sedimentary rock was upturned when
forces within the earth began pushing up and creating
the Rocky Mountains to the east. Courtesy of National
Park Service, U.S. Department of the Interior.*

# The Morrison Formation

The third locality, in addition to the deposits of Holzmaden and Solnhofen, from which Jurassic fossils of Carnegie Museum of Natural History's collection were taken is the famous Morrison Formation located in the western United States. Laid down in the latter part of the Jurassic, approximately 140 to 135 million years ago, the Morrison Formation is a complex series of interbedded sandstones, mudstones, gravelly sands and fresh water limestones left in a flat basin when the Sundance Sea withdrew to the North. As previously mentioned, this Jurassic formation occurs at Dinosaur National Monument.

Geologic evidence indicates that during the Jurassic, the Rocky Mountain area was a broad floodplain covered by forests containing a variety of conifers, ginkgo trees, ferns, and bennettites (trees resembling stubby palms with the addition of a flower-like reproductive structure on their trunks). The year 'round climate was warm but not necessarily humid.

A shallow river, originating in the mountains far to the west, maintained a continuous flow. Often, its streams were full and spread out over the floodplains, depositing loads of silt. Complete and partial dinosaur carcasses and bones washed into stream channels; a few became lodged on a late Jurassic sandbar which today is an extraordinary exhibit at Dinosaur National Monument.

The placement of the long necks and tails of the fossil sauropod skeletons found at Dinosaur National Monument demonstrate the direction of the flow of the ancient stream running through the area. The small *Camarasaurus* on display in Dinosaur Hall, for instance, shown in almost the same position as it was found, apparently floated downstream and lodged crosswise on the sandbar; the eastward-flowing current moved the long neck and tail to the downstream side. Other more or less complete vertebral columns of sauropods in the quarry were also found aligned toward the east.

# Some Reptiles from the Morrison Formation

Besides dinosaurs, two kinds of crocodilians were found in the Morrison Formation at Dinosaur National Monument. *Goniopholis* resembled the modern-day crocodile in size. The other crocodilian, *Hoplosuchus,* was tiny in comparison. It belongs to a family of late Jurassic crocodilians that, as adults, were less than a foot (30.5 cm) long. The nearly complete *Hoplosuchus kayi* in Carnegie Museum's collection is about 7 inches (18 cm) long. In life, with the full length of its tail, *Hoplosuchus* probably measured about 8 inches (20 cm).

From the Carnegie specimen, *Hoplosuchus'* short, broad skull can be identified. Although paired armor plates lying under the skin are prominent in *Hoplosuchus,* the armor that covered the rest of the body was scant in comparison to that found on most crocodilians.

# Dinosaurs from the Morrison Formation

Single dinosaur bones are widespread in the Morrison Formation, but only six concentrations of thousands of bones, accumulated under varying conditions in restricted areas, have been described. At one of these sites, Dinosaur National Monument, approximately 5000 bones have been uncovered since Earl Douglass' discovery of *Apatosaurus* in 1909. Here, the uncovered dinosaurs include at least sixty different individuals representing at least ten different types.

Two of the six concentrations are located in the Como Bluff area of southeastern Wyoming near the town of Medicine Bow. Bone Cabin Quarry, from which American Museum of Natural History field crews removed an estimated 6000 bones between 1898 and 1903, accumulated in a river channel smaller than the one at Dinosaur National Monument. Quarry 13, worked between 1879 and 1887 under the direction of O.C. Marsh

Distribution of the Morrison Formation and some of its principal dinosaur localities:
1. Dinosaur National Monument
2. Como Bluff Region, including Bone Cabin Quarry and Quarry 13
3. Howe Quarry, located in the central part of the Bighorn Basin
4. Cleveland-Lloyd Quarry
5. Sheep Creek

of the Peabody Museum of Natural History, produced approximately 3000 bones. These were mainly the bones of smaller dinosaurs, bones that seem to have been deposited on a floodplain behind a natural levee during periods of high water.

The fourth concentration of bones in the Morrison Formation was found at Howe Quarry in northern Wyoming. An extremely dense accumulation of about 4000 bones, the deposit included many strings of vertebrae, a few limb bones, and twelve articulated feet and legs preserved in an upright position. Apparently, the dinosaurs of this area became mired in mud near a river and perished. Scavengers and decay dismembered most of the carcasses, but some legs remained in position.

The fifth major bone quarry of the Morrison Formation, the Cleveland-Lloyd Quarry in central Utah, contained 10,000 bones, mostly of *Allosaurus*. These bones were trapped in an oxbow lake. Only isolated, partial skeletons come from the sixth site, the Sheep Creek Quarry. Here, the skeletons composing Carnegie Museum of Natural History's mounted *Diplodocus* were excavated.

All together, eighteen different types of dinosaurs are known from a total of nineteen separate localities in the Morrison Formation. Others will probably be added to the list when collections from several sites in western Colorado discovered since 1960 are fully prepared and described.

Of those dinosaurs found in the Morrison Formation, *Camarasaurus, Allosaurus, Apatosaurus, Diplodocus,* and *Stegosaurus* have been the most common; their remains have been found in the greatest number of sites. Of these, *Camarasaurus* is the most abundant dinosaur, with two or more individuals typically found at a particular site. *Diplodocus* and *Apatosaurus,* respectively, represent the second and third most frequently found dinosaurs in individual sites. Fewer *Allosaurus* specimens are generally found than the other four dinosaurs.

The ratio of dinosaur types found in the Morrison Formation is consistent with facts known of their habits. Predators, for instance, are generally less common than their prey; sauropods, plant-eating dinosaurs such as *Camarasaurus, Diplodocus,* and *Apatosaurus,* therefore,

are more abundant than their theropod predators such as *Allosaurus.*

All five dinosaurs mentioned above can be seen in Dinosaur Hall. In addition to these, two other dinosaurs found in the Morrison Formation are on display: the relatively small Jurassic herbivores *Dryosaurus* and *Camptosaurus.*

Other dinosaurs, in addition to those on display here, have been found in the Morrison Formation. These have included a number of theropods—small, bipedal predators averaging from 6 through 15 feet (1.8-4.6 m) in length. The scanty number of these predatory dinosaurs is not unexpected.

In addition to *Allosaurus,* the remains of one other large predator have been uncovered in the Morrison Formation. Two fragments of this dinosaur, *Ceratosaurus,* are in the collections here but are not on display. Somewhat similar in appearance but smaller than *Allosaurus, Ceratosaurus* had a single small horn on its snout.

Some lesser known dinosaurs found in the Morrison Formation's Jurassic rock were similar in appearance to more familiar forms: *Barosaurus,* a rarely found dinosaur, is typical of sauropods such as *Diplodocus. Othnielia* is thought to have been similar to *Dryosaurus* in appearance. The largest known dinosaur, *Brachiosaurus,* is represented in the Morrison Formation by only two partial skeletons. The tiny, bipedal *Nanosaurus,* also found in the Morrison Formation, was only 4½ feet (1.4 m).

# *Allosaurus*, the Theropod Predator

The plant-eating dinosaurs that lived in the vicinity of Dinosaur National Monument had one particularly formidable enemy, *Allosaurus.* Although other flesh-eating dinosaurs existed, *Allosaurus* was the largest and most abundant. Its remains have been discovered in at least eleven localities in the Morrison Formation. Similar dinosaurs come from late Jurassic and early Cretaceous deposits in eastern Asia, eastern Africa, and western Europe.

Allosaurus fragilis *(C.M. Vertebrate Fossil No. 11844 and casts of U.U. 6000 and U.S.N.M. 4734) from the Carnegie Museum Quarry in the Morrison Formation, Dinosaur National Monument, Utah.* Allosaurus, *a large and abundant theropod predator of the late Jurassic, was about 35 feet long as an adult. Its jaws were armed with numerous serrated teeth for ripping and slicing flesh. Its long tail, which served as a counterbalancing device, was held off the ground while walking.*

*Top:* Allosaurus fragilis *skull (C.M. Vertebrate Fossil No. 11844 and cast of skull U.U. 6000). This ferocious dinosaur's mouth was lined with sharp, serrated teeth. Once its prey was overcome,* Allosaurus *could extend its jaws to swallow chunks of meat larger than its normal mouth size.* **Bottom left:** *Forelimbs of* Allosaurus fragilis *(C.M. Vertebrate Fossil No. 11844 and forelimbs cast from U.S.N.M. 4734), a late Jurassic carnivore. The three fingers of each forelimb ended in long, sharp claws which were used in ripping and grasping prey.*

**Bottom right:** *Foot of* Allosaurus fragilis *(C.M. Vertebrate Fossil No. 11844), an early carnivore. The powerful hind legs of this dinosaur terminated in bird-like feet, each with four toes. The smaller, backward-pointing toe corresponds to a human's big toe.*

Adult allosaurs from Dinosaur National Monument measured about 35 feet (10.7 m) from the tip of the snout to the end of the tail. Fragmentary remains from Utah's Cleveland-Lloyd Quarry show that some allosaurs grew almost as large as *Tyrannosaurus.* In contrast, the smallest allosaurs uncovered in Dinosaur National Monument were about 9 feet 10 inches (3 m) long and stood about 3 feet 4 inches (1 m) high.

*Allosaurus* had a huge mouth armed with pointed, curved teeth up to 3 inches (7.6 cm) long. As in most theropods, the front and back of each of *Allosaurus'* teeth were lined with tiny serrations. Resembling the serrations on steak knives, they served the same function: With them the tooth could slice through skin and flesh quite efficiently.

One would expect that a skull the size of *Allosaurus'* would be difficult for the rest of the body to support. As pointed out earlier in the chapter "What is a Dinosaur?," openings in the large skull of the dinosaurs greatly reduced its overall weight without reducing its strength. Also, the vertebrae in *Allosaurus'* neck were short, a modification that allowed the weight of the large head to be supported.

Like modern lizards and snakes, *Allosaurus* could swallow objects larger than its regular mouth size. Bones in the roof of its mouth and lower jaw had a certain looseness to them that permitted the mouth to open larger than normal when the dinosaur swallowed a particularly large object.

*Allosaurus'* front legs were too short to be used in walking; except when *Allosaurus* was resting, these legs rarely touched the ground. In contrast, *Allosaurus'* hind legs and hip bones were very powerful because they had to support the entire weight of the beast. The hind legs terminated in bird-like feet with three long toes pointing forward and another much smaller toe (corresponding to the big toe of humans) pointing inward and slightly backward. Like birds and many of today's mammals, *Allosaurus* walked on the balls of its feet. The three long bones (metatarsals) to which the toes attached corresponded to the elongated bones between the heel and the ball of a human foot. In *Allosaurus,* these bones formed the lower segment of the leg.

The small but sturdy hands of *Allosaurus* had three fingers, each armed with a powerful claw. *Allosaurus* probably attacked its victims with a terrifying combination of slashing teeth and ripping, grasping claws.

The tail was long and heavy, with the vertebrae firmly interlocked so that the tail was capable of little up and down movement. It served as a counter-balance to the weight of the head, and was held well off the ground when the animal walked. The proportions of the hind legs indicate that *Allosaurus* was not a speedy animal. In life it may have stepped deliberately along, rocking from side to side, its head thrusting back and forth with each step.

*Allosaurus* probably preyed upon any dinosaur it could catch and overpower. Medium-sized dinosaurs like *Camptosaurus* and slow-moving *Stegosaurus,* as well as immature sauropods such as the young *Camarasaurus* may have been especially vulnerable. Fast dinosaurs like *Dryosaurus* probably could have easily outrun an adult *Allosaurus.*

Could *Allosaurus* kill a huge, fully grown sauropod such as *Diplodocus* or *Apatosaurus*? Evidently, it did feed on them; a series of *Apatosaurus* vertebrae at the American Museum of Natural History have many tooth marks that coincide well with the size and spacing of *Allosaurus'* teeth. Did the allosaur kill the unfortunate dinosaur or was it already dead from some other cause? This is unknown. *Allosaurus* was a large and formidable beast, but an adult sauropod weighed five to thirty times as much. When *Allosaurus* came upon one on dry land, it had to take care that the sauropod's great tail did not send it flying head over heels.

Some people have conjectured that if sauropods such as *Diplodocus* and other plant-eating dinosaurs retreated to deep water, they were safe from hungry theropods such as *Allosaurus*. Sets of footprints recently discovered in the early Jurassic rocks at Connecticut State Dinosaur Park, Rocky Hill, provide evidence that this may not have been the case. Most of the unusual prints were apparently made by large theropods that had been floating or were half submerged, pushing themselves along the bottom with the tips of their toes. One set of the semi-swimming prints was made by a small dinosaur thought to resemble *Coelophysis*. The tracks indicate that both large and small theropods may have been competent swimmers, capable of pursuing their prey into fairly deep water.

Possibly *Allosaurus* and other carnivorous dinosaurs sometimes hunted together in loosely organized groups. If so, they could have ganged up on adult sauropods and successfully killed them. This seems a reasonable possibility since many modern-day meat-eating mammals have learned to cooperate in packs and regularly kill animals larger than any one of the predators individually. A wolf pack, for instance, can kill a moose that no single wolf would stand a chance of slaughtering.

Occasionally, the fossil remains of carnivorous dinosaurs are found in groups. The Cleveland-Lloyd Quarry has yielded the remains of at least forty-four allosaurs, more than all the plant-eating dinosaurs found in this location combined. Possibly, this unusual concentration of predators was the result of a "predator trap" where carnivorous dinosaurs were lured to their deaths, one by one, by the sight of a prey species already ensnared in the trap. The huge quantity of skeletons, on the other hand, might have been the result of some unknown, natural catastrophe.

Carnegie Museum of Natural History's mounted *Allosaurus* is largely derived from a single, relatively complete skeleton excavated by Earl Douglass and his field crews between 1913 and 1915. The skull found with the skeleton was incomplete. When the *Allosaurus* skeleton was mounted, this skull was replaced by a cast of a better one from the University of Utah's collection. The forelimbs of the *Allosaurus* skeleton

also are casts taken from a skeleton belonging to a different museum, Smithsonian Institution. The mount was assembled and put on display at Carnegie Museum in 1938.

# The Sauropod Dinosaurs

Most people are probably more familiar with the sauropod dinosaurs than they are with most kinds of modern animals. A gigantic, long-necked, long-tailed beast resembling a sauropod served as the symbol of a major oil company for years. Sauropods are also familiar to viewers of Saturday morning television and the movies. Fred Flintstone keeps one as a pet, and King Kong has battled them on a mysterious, lost island. Popular treatments aside, there is no evidence that they survived later than 65 million years ago. No human—not even the cartoon character Fred Flintstone—would have ever seen one alive.

The oldest true sauropods are known from the late Triassic to the early Jurassic, while the most recent are known from the end of the Cretaceous. This represents a span of about 147 million years. During the late Jurassic and early Cretaceous, the sauropods reached their peak of abundance and diversity.

### The History of the Sauropods

As mentioned in an earlier chapter, sauropod dinosaurs are believed to have evolved from ancestral reptiles called thecodonts. An early theory maintained that, like the thecodonts, sauropods were originally small, bipedal dinosaurs with long necks, small heads and small, pointed teeth. By the end of the Triassic, the ancestral sauropods are thought to have become larger with longer necks, smaller heads and peg-like teeth. According to this theory, these dinosaurs evolved into the large prosauropods and later into the even larger sauropods. With their increased size, the sauropods were unable to walk solely on two feet; they became quadrupedal to accommodate their greater body weight. The fact that the forelegs of most sauropods are shorter than their hind legs has been cited as proof of their bipedal ancestry.

Recently, others have challenged this theory. These scientists contend that the hypothesized transitional sequence from bipedal to quadrupedal forms is not supported by evidence from the fossil record; the difference in size between sauropods' front and back legs does not indicate that they were once bipedal. This current theory generally regards thecodonts as bipedal, but those from which the sauropods were derived are believed to have been quadrupedal. It is thought that the quadrupedal thecodonts were an even earlier form of thecodont than the bipedal form.

Despite the difference in leg length of the sauropods, when standing on all fours, their backs were essentially horizontal. It is argued that there was no advantage to having front legs of the same length as the back legs.

Sauropods were most prevalent from the late Jurassic to the early Cretaceous. During this span of time, they were probably common throughout the world. Later in the Cretaceous Period, the number of sauropods in the northern hemisphere began to decline, even though they were still fairly abundant but not as diverse in the southern hemisphere. Sauropods were present but rare in North America during the late Cretaceous.

At about the time the sauropods began to wane, another group of plant-eating dinosaurs, the hadrosaurs (or duckbills) appeared and began a rapid increase in diversity and numbers. Although not as large as the sauropods, the hadrosaurs were better swimmers, fleeter of foot, had keener senses, and excellent, well-adapted teeth. These teeth were well-suited for chewing more modern types of plants that were also gaining dominance at the time. Perhaps the hadrosaurs were actually better adapted to the late Cretaceous environment and thus displaced the sauropods from most of their habitats.

### How Big Did the Sauropods Grow?

Sauropods are the largest animals known to have walked on earth, even though only a few known skeletons of adults are complete enough to provide approximate measurements of overall

lengths. From these skeletons it is estimated that the sauropods ranged from about 43 feet (13 m) to 84 feet (26 m). These measurements are based upon the shortest known sauropod—*Dicraeosaurus,* a *Diplodocus*-like dinosaur from the late Jurassic of eastern Africa—to the longest—*Diplodocus,* from the late Jurassic of North America.

Although *Diplodocus* is the longest dinosaur documented, it was outweighed by several shorter but bulkier sauropods. *Brachiosaurus* is the largest sauropod about which an adequate amount of information is known. Its remains have been found in late Jurassic sediments of North America and of Tendaguru, Tanzania, in eastern Africa. Unusual among dinosaurs because its front legs were longer than the hind legs, this short-tailed, long-necked giant was almost as long as *Diplodocus* and is estimated to have weighed a staggering 86 tons (78,000 kg). Standing on all four feet, its head was 40 feet (12 m) in the air.

In 1972, the partial skeleton of a possibly larger sauropod was discovered in an exposure of the Morrison Formation on the west slope of the Rocky Mountains in southwestern Colorado. The two bones making up this dinosaur's shoulder girdle are 8 feet (2.4 m) long, a sizable increase over the 6½ foot (2 m) length in *Apatosaurus.* Its neck vertebrae are up to 5 feet (1.5 m) long. The skeleton has not yet been described in scientific literature, but the animal may possibly be related to *Brachiosaurus.* Whether or not it will displace *Brachiosaurus* as the heaviest known dinosaur remains to be seen.

### Why Were the Sauropods So Large?

One of the main advantages of being a giant has already been mentioned in the chapter "Were the Dinosaurs Warm-Blooded?" Whether or not sauropods were endotherms, warmed by their own metabolic heat, their size permitted them to maintain a relatively constant body temperature without an insulating coat of hair or feathers. Unlike modern reptiles, adult sauropods probably could be relatively active day or night.

Another advantage sauropods gained by their size is that it discouraged predators. It is doubtful that a single allosaur, one of the largest predators of its time, for instance, could have brought down a healthy adult sauropod.

A giant requires much food, but, also because of its size, it could obtain food from a variety of places. The sauropods could reach far beneath the surface of a lake or river or as far up as the tops of tall trees. Extremely tall trees could be knocked down for more convenient consumption.

## The Problems of Being a Giant

Despite the advantages, there are also drawbacks to being extremely large. As the external dimensions of an animal increase, its volume and weight increase much faster. If the length of an animal is doubled, for example, while body proportions remain the same, the animal's weight is cubed. The heavier the animal, the more gravity becomes a problem. A fly, for instance, can almost ignore gravity whereas a man cannot. Humans can jump or fall several feet without injury; an elephant cannot jump at all.

The sauropod skeleton evolved so that the weight-bearing portions were as strong as possible while those portions not bearing weight were light yet strong. Sauropods' leg bones are, thus, solid, pillar-like structures capable of holding up the tons of flesh pressing down upon them. Fossil trackways show that sauropods kept their legs nearly straight when they walked, as do elephants, so that the axes of the legs were aligned against the pull of gravity.

As a result of evolutionary changes, sauropods had fewer toe bones than their predecessors. The remaining toe bones were short and stubby and encased in cushioned pads. The feet, which made oval footprints, resembled those of the hippopotamus or rhinoceros. The inner toes of sauropods from the Jurassic were armed with stout claws.

The greatest part of the sauropods' weight was borne on the hind legs and the pelvis. The sauropod pelvis represents perhaps the strongest complex of bone evolved in any animal. The front legs also bore considerable weight. They were connected to the body by four to six shoulder bones that formed a kind of U-shaped sling

around the lower front of the body. The proportions of the legs and the rigidity of the shoulder bones suggest that sauropods walked very slowly.

The vertebrae of the neck in some sauropods tend to have twice the number of linkages found in most animals with backbones. They made the spine rigid and better able to resist the downward pull of the body. To reduce the weight of the backbone as much as possible without significantly weakening it, the portions of each vertebra not subject to stress were hollowed out, leaving a set of struts and braces.

The vertebrae between the shoulder blades and on forward to just behind the skull are unusual in some sauropods. Each of the vertical spines is divided, forming a long trough down the back of the neck. Visitors to Carnegie Museum of Natural History can clearly see this trough by looking down on *Diplodocus* from the balcony on the second floor above Dinosaur Hall. A great ligament ran through the trough, fastening just behind the head. It helped the sauropod to move its head and neck up and down, functioning like the cable in a crane or power shovel as it raises and lowers the boom.

## Heads and Tails

An isolated sauropod skull is large, yet, in place on the skeleton, it looks ridiculously small. Sauropod skulls have a variety of shapes; those of *Camarasaurus* and *Diplodocus* illustrate two extremes. *Camarasaurus* has a short snout, and, when viewed from the side, its skull appears almost round. *Diplodocus,* on the other hand, has an elongated, rather horse-like profile. In all known sauropods, the nostrils are not at the end of the snout but rather far back on the forehead, just in front of the eyes.

In *Camarasaurus,* the teeth are set both along the sides of the jaws and in the front of the mouth. *Diplodocus'* teeth grew only in the front of the mouth and slanted forward; they are slender and more or less rounded in cross section. As in all dinosaurs, the teeth were regularly replaced by new ones that grew up into the roots of the old teeth.

*Top: Skull of adult* Camarasaurus lentus *(C.M. Vertebrate Fossil No. 12020). Large nostril openings are high on the skull of this short-snouted sauropod dinosaur.* Camarasaurus' *spoon-shaped teeth, used for eating plant material, were continuously replaced throughout its lifetime. Bottom:* Diplodocus *skull (C.M. Vertebrate Fossil No. 11161). Some have speculated that the slender, pencil-like teeth lining the front of* Diplodocus' *mouth were used to pluck molluscs and other forms of aquatic life from river and lake bottoms.*

At the opposite end of the sauropod was a long, heavy tail. In *Diplodocus, Apatosaurus,* and closely related dinosaurs, the end of the tail was drawn out into a long, very slender whiplash composed of thin, rodlike bones. Some paleontologists think this whiplash of a tail was used to deliver powerful wallops to attacking predators and other foes. The tail may also have been used in swimming, although it probably was not as effective as the flattened tails of the duck-billed and crested dinosaurs.

Also unlike the duck-billed dinosaurs and theropod dinosaurs, sauropods' tails were not stiffened with bony rods. Duckbills and theropods almost certainly held their tails off the ground when they walked, but sauropod specialists are not sure if sauropods did the same. Sauropod trackways from the early Cretaceous found in central Texas show that they sometimes dragged their tails. Most other trackways, however, do not have drag marks, and, possibly, the dinosaurs responsible for these trackways were walking in water deep enough to support their tails.

Notice the tail vertebrae in the mounted skeletons of *Apatosaurus* and *Diplodocus* in Dinosaur Hall. Two tail vertebrae near or just above the point where the tail reached the ground are joined together by a rough, bony swelling, indicating a form of arthritis. Other sauropod skeletons also show evidence of this kind of arthritis *(spondylitis deformans)* caused by some injury or strain on the tail.

**The Life of a Sauropod: Aquatic, Terrestrial, or Both?**

Because no animals even remotely similar to sauropods are alive today, paleontologists run into problems when they try to reconstruct the habits, diets, and appearance of the dinosaurs. Until recently, sauropods were usually pictured as being aquatic or semi-aquatic. Some people speculated that they were so heavy that they had to stay in the water where their heavy bodies were bouyed up.

The notion that sauropods were aquatic appears to have originated in 1841. This is when Sir Richard Owen described the fragmentary remains of *Cetiosaurus*, the first known sauropod from the late Jurassic of southern England. Owen believed the dinosaur to be a kind of large crocodilian. He considered the bone in the dinosaur's legs to be whale-like in size and named the dinosaur *"Cetiosaurus"* ("whale reptile") as a result.

After 1841, a few other sauropods were named on the basis of fragments found in other localities. Then, beginning in 1877, the famous rival paleontologists, Cope and Marsh, started describing new sauropods based on more complete remains found in Wyoming and Colorado. (Refer to "The History of the Mesozoic Collection at Carnegie Museum of Natural History" for more information on the work of Cope and Marsh.) At first, both men assumed the new dinosaurs were terrestrial. Both, however, later reversed their opinions and supported the theory that sauropods were aquatic or at least amphibious. It has been speculated that, at the time, Owen was so influential that both American scientists changed their thinking when their studies showed that *Cetiosaurus* and their new sauropods were similar.

To substantiate further their shifts in opinion, Cope and Marsh pointed out that the position of sauropods' nostrils on top of the head was convincing evidence that sauropods spent much of their lives with their heads under water and with only their eyes and nostrils above the water-line. On the one hand, many kinds of extinct aquatic reptiles (such as nothosaurs and ichthyosaurs) and modern-day aquatic mammals (such as whales and porpoises) do have nostrils back near their eyes. On the other hand, however, some land mammals such as elephants and tapirs have their nostril openings high on their skulls, both in connection with a flexible proboscis. Many aquatic mammals and reptiles have nostrils in the "normal" position—at the end of the snout. These include sea turtles, seals, crocodilians, and hippopotamuses. With lack of clear evidence, it would seem that the position of sauropods' nostrils does not necessarily serve as an indication that sauropods were aquatic.

A team of paleontologists interested in the question of whether sauropods were primarily aquatic or terrestrial has studied localities in the Morrison Formation. According to their interpretations sauropods from the Morrison Formation appear to have been terrestrial but frequent visitors to the water, as are the elephants and moose of today.

Footprints left in the sauropod trackway found in central Texas also seem to lend support to their finding. As noted earlier, it has been suggested that many of the dinosaurs that produced the trackway were walking in water deep enough to support their tails. Tracks from one sauropod further suggest that this dinosaur was walking in deep water. From the footprints it would appear that the sauropod walked on forefeet, with its hind legs and tail floating behind. A single hind foot impression at one point seems to indicate that, upon making a turn, the dinosaur put down one hind leg and pushed off.

**Food for the Sauropods**

Despite the sketchy picture of where the sauropods lived, there is even less evidence as to what they ate. Thus far, only one indication concerning the sauropod diet exists. In the early 1960s, a badly weathered sauropod skeleton was found in a cliff of Morrison Formation sediments. At the approximate position where the stomach would have been was found a strange mass composed of lumps of clay, pieces of twigs and branches, substances that may have once been plant remains, and cavities that could have once been gas bubbles. More surprisingly, several poorly preserved pieces of bones and a single *Allosaurus* tooth were found in the stomach region. Due to severe weathering, it was impossible to tell what kind of sauropod it was; this dinosaur, nonetheless, was not particular about what it ate. Perhaps its last meal was dredged up from a muddy river bottom rich in carrion and other organic material. It is known that sauropods had tongues because the small bones from the base of the tongue have sometimes been found. Paleontologists speculate that the mouth of sauropod dinosaurs may have held a long, flexible tongue, like a cow's, which would have been useful for gathering tufts of leaves and grass and pulling them loose. Perhaps a proboscis like that of the elephant or tapir may have been present.

How much did a sauropod eat? It has been estimated that an *Apatosaurus* needed 1¾ tons (1600 kg) of green plant food each day. To obtain such huge quantities of food, sauropods, like elephants of today, very likely broke down trees, trampled the underbrush, and otherwise had a profound effect on their surroundings. Also like elephants, they may have had to roam widely, constantly searching for new food supplies.

Sauropod teeth were obviously not those of a predator. Neither could they have been used for chewing up the leaves and twigs that probably composed the bulk of their diet. The pencil-like teeth of *Diplodocus,* for example, are known to have worn like a piece of chalk held vertically against a blackboard. If this sauropod's teeth were used to rake in plant material, it would be difficult to explain such wear on the teeth. Perhaps *Diplodocus* used its teeth to pluck clams or other molluscs from the river and lake bottoms; the wear on its teeth would be more consistent with this explanation. Unlike the teeth of *Diplodocus,* however, *Camarasaurus'* teeth wore along the edge. Perhaps *Camarasaurus'* teeth were worn down through the continual stripping of leaves from tree branches.

If sauropods could not use their teeth to chew, how could they digest their food? Some scientists think that, like birds, dinosaurs had a gizzard— a muscular, internal organ filled with small rocks. The rocks would have ground the food before it entered the stomach.

Throughout the West, collectors often find rounded, highly polished stones. While some occur in Mesozoic rocks, others have been found in sediments where no dinosaurs would be found. Some scientists have assumed that such rocks were once in the gizzards of dinosaurs. Most of these rocks were almost certainly produced by the action of high-velocity winds carrying abrasive sand grains.

Whether or not sauropods had gizzards, their digestive tracts must have been equipped in some way to cope with huge quantities of unchewed plant material. Perhaps, instead of a gizzard, sauropods depended on bacteria to break down the cellulose in their digestive tracts.

### Reproduction and Sauropod Young

Visitors of the Museum often ask how the sauropods reproduced. Unfortunately, not enough good sauropod skeletons have been found to be able to distinguish males from females. Thus far, no evidence of reproductive organs has been found either. It is known, however, that some sauropods laid eggs. Many basketball-sized, round eggs, some seemingly laid and preserved in clutches, have been discovered in late Cretaceous sediments in southern France. In these same deposits, bones of the 39 foot (12 m) long sauropod *Hypselosaurus* have turned up. Although the eggs in the deposits are varied in size and shape, it seems reasonable to credit *Hypelosaurus* as the largest.

Several skeletons of immature dinosaurs are known, but the only remains of very young dinosaurs were discovered in 1977 in late Triassic deposits in Patgonia, Argentina. The skeletons of at least six robin-sized dinosaurs associated with two eggs, were recovered from a nest. These babies were probably distantly related to the prosauropod *Plateosaurus*.

### Group Behavior

Evidence from the sauropod trackways has been used to suggest that sauropods not only frequented water, as previously mentioned, but also may have traveled in small groups or even herds. The tracks of twenty-three sauropods, found in southern Texas, suggest that the dinosaurs moved at a leisurely pace like cows going down a country lane. All were traveling in the same direction, and it is thought they were moving in a single herd.

## Carnegie's Sauropods

Three sauropods—*Camarasaurus, Diplodocus,* and *Apatosaurus*—dominate the Jurassic displays in Dinosaur Hall.

### *Camarasaurus*

Two specimens of *Camarasaurus* are on view in Dinosaur Hall, the skull of an adult and the nearly complete skeleton of an immature individual. (The skeleton associated with the adult skull is kept in storage because present exhibit space is too limited for it to be on display.) The immature *Camarasaurus* on exhibit is perhaps the most complete sauropod skeleton ever found. The skeleton is displayed almost as it was originally discovered. Only the left hind leg and the left half of the pelvis were restored with bones from another individual. When the immature *Camarasaurus* was found, its tail was bent forward to touch the back of the neck; the tail was straightened for exhibit purposes.

Camarasaurus lentus *(C.M. Vertebrate Fossil No. 11338), a quadrupedal sauropod dinosaur from the Jurassic Morrison Formation, Dinosaur National Monument. This immature individual is one of the most complete sauropod skeletons ever found. In an adult* Camarasaurus, *the neck and tail are proportionately longer.*

Carnegie Museum's young *Camarasaurus* skeleton is unusually complete. Museum visitors, accustomed to seeing complete skeletons, may assume that most fossil vertebrates are found intact. This is not the case. Between the time they died and the time they were safely buried and on their way to becoming fossils, sauropods such as *Camarasaurus* were particularly liable to dismemberment. The skulls were loosely attached and almost always came off. Scavengers and water currents took apart the remaining portions. A paleontologist is happy to discover partial skeletal associations. Much more frequently, only single bones are found, representing both different individuals and different kinds of dinosaurs.

The Museum's immature *Camarasaurus* is characterized by a relatively short neck and large head, typical of a sauropod youngster. If it had lived to adulthood, its neck would have grown proportionately longer, although, like its tail, the neck would never be as long as that of the larger, more specialized *Diplodocus* and *Apatosaurus.*

Unlike the contemporary *Diplodocus* and *Apatosaurus, Camarasaurus* had short, undivided spines of the vertebrae. Its snout was short, and it had large openings for the nostrils high on the skull just in front of the eyes. Again, unlike *Diplodocus* and *Apatosaurus, Camarasaurus'* forelegs were relatively long, about four-fifths the length of the hind legs. With its longer forelegs, *Camarasaurus'* back was more horizontal than that of these other sauropods, which were higher over the hips.

A somewhat larger *Camarasaurus* skeleton is in Yale's Peabody Museum of Natural History at New Haven, Connecticut, and another, about half grown, is exhibited at the Smithsonian Institution in Washington, D.C. Perhaps, because these well-known skeletons are all immature, people tend to assume that *Camarasaurus* was a small sauropod. Actually, some adult *Camarasaurus are known to have been as large as Apatosaurus.*

*Camarasaurus* is the most abundant dinosaur in the Morrison Formation. The common occurrence of two or more *Camarasaurus* individuals preserved together may indicate that it was a gregarious dinosaur.

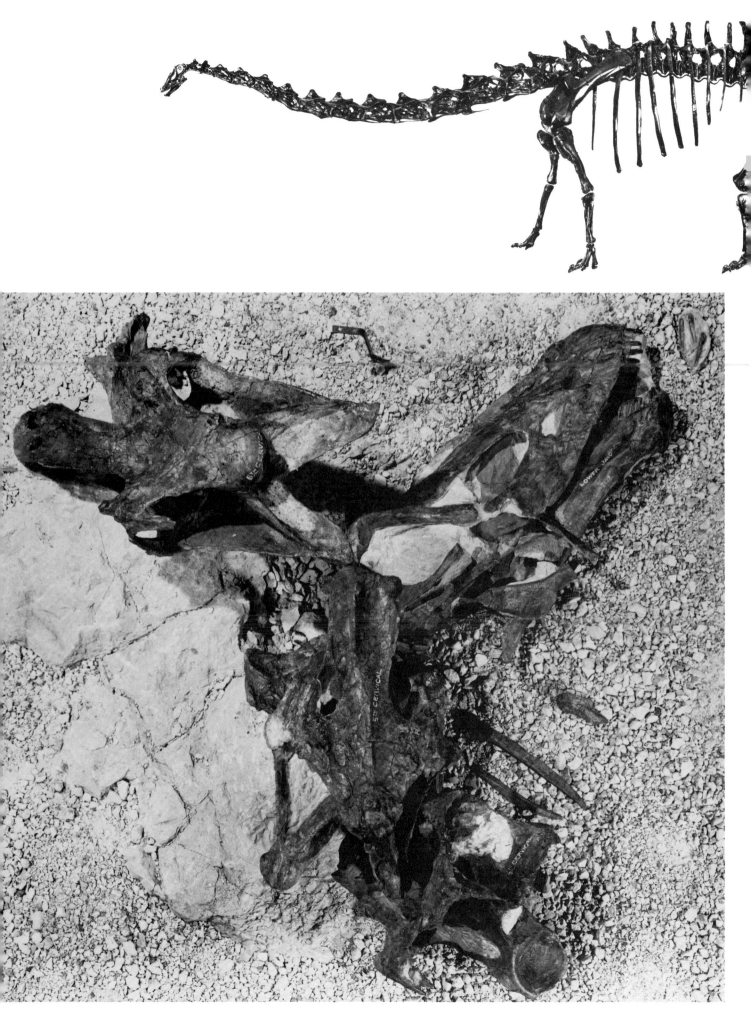

Diplodocus carnegii *(C.M. Vertebrate Fossil No. 84, 94 and 307; skull based upon C.M. Vertebrate Fossil No. 662 and U.S.N.M. 2673). As the first dinosaur discovered by Carnegie Museum,* Diplodocus carnegii *played a vital role in establishing the Museum as a center for studying and collecting dinosaurs. Numerous casts of this dinosaur stand in museums throughout the world. At 84 feet, it is the longest known dinosaur.*

## Diplodocus

*Diplodocus* follows *Camarasaurus* in abundance in the Morrison Formation. Like *Camarasaurus,* the remains of several *Diplodocus* tend to be found together. Five incomplete skeletons and much fragmentary material has been collected, making *Diplodocus* relatively well known. Probably related dinosaurs with somewhat similar skulls and slender, but less peg-like, teeth have also been found in Africa and Mongolia.

*Diplodocus* is the longest dinosaur known. With the entire length of its whip-like tail, Carnegie's "Dippy" actually measures 84 feet (25.6 m). The mounted dinosaur stands 14 feet 8 inches (4.5 m) high at the hips. With its slender build, extremely long neck, and short body, *Diplodocus* is estimated to have weighed about twelve tons (11,000 kg), only about one-third as much as an adult *Apatosaurus.*

*Diplodocus'* skull bones are notably thin and fragile for such an enormous creature. The nostrils are placed on the forehead of its long-snouted skull, just in front of the eyes. The slender, forward-slanting teeth grew only in the front of the mouth.

The story of how Carnegie's "Dippy" was discovered, excavated and mounted was told earlier in this book ("Andrew Carnegie's Gift"). The two partial skeletons from Sheep Creek, Wyoming, comprising most of the mounted skeleton, had incomplete tails. In 1903, a Carnegie Museum field party found the back half of a *Diplodocus* tail along the Red Fork of the Powder River about 100 miles (161 km) north of Sheep Creek. The find showed that *Diplodocus* had a whiplash tail, and the tail was subsequently incorporated into the mount.

Parts from five other sauropods have also been incorporated into the mounted *Diplodocus.* The skull is modeled after two partial skulls. The left hind foot is from a partial *Diplodocus* skeleton collected by Carnegie Museum at Sheep Creek, Wyoming, and the left foreleg comes from another dinosaur in the Museum's collection. The forefeet are based on those of a much larger specimen from the American Museum of Natural History. Although once attributed to *Diplodocus,* the forefeet and left foreleg are now known to belong to *Camarasaurus.*

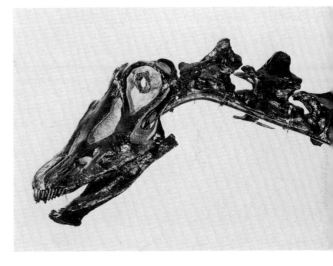

*Above:* Diplodocus carnegii *(Based on C.M. Vertebrate Fossil Nos. 84, 662 and U.S.N.M. 2673). A surprisingly small skull sits atop the body of this, the longest of dinosaurs.* Diplodocus' *skull bones are also notably thin and fragile for such an enormous creature.*

*Page 68:* Diplodocus carnegii *(C.M. Vertebrate Fossil No. 3452). Unless a dinosaur skull is found in close association with the rest of the skeleton, it is often difficult to determine which skull belongs to a particular dinosaur. This* Diplodocus *skull is shown as it was actually found along with several neck vertebrae.*

Apatosaurus louisae *(C.M. Vertebrate Fossil Nos. 3018 and 11162), the most perfect specimen of this dinosaur ever collected. Discovered by Earl Douglass in 1909,* Apatosaurus *was the first of a long list of dinosaurs taken from the area now known as Dinosaur National Monument. It has been estimated that, in life, this approximately 35-ton giant consumed 1¾ tons of plant material each day.*

**Left:** *Installing* Apatosaurus louisae *at Carnegie Museum. Taken around 1915, this picture shows Douglass' initial find being mounted for exhibition. At the time of its installation,* Apatosaurus louisae *was the most perfect of the four specimens mounted in the United States museums.* **Above:** *Carnegie Museum's* Apatosaurus *skeleton remained headless for more than twenty years. After the death of W.J. Holland, a cast of an adult* Camarasaurus *skull was placed on the* Apatosaurus *skeleton despite the controversy over its being the correct skull. Not until 1979 was the* Camarasaurus *skull replaced with the correct head.*

## Apatosaurus

The name *"Brontosaurus,"* meaning "thunder lizard," is probably more widely known than any other dinosaur name. Although popularly known as *"Brontosaurus,"* this dinosaur's correct scientific name is *Apatosaurus* (meaning "false lizard"), the name coined by O.C. Marsh for the first dinosaur of this type discovered. Not knowing that they were actually larger examples of the same dinosaur, Marsh later named the dinosaurs *"Brontosaurus."* It was then discovered that *"Brontosaurus"* and *Apatosaurus* were actually the same dinosaurs. According to the rules governing the assignment of scientific names, the name first assigned takes precedence. Thus, the name *"Apatosaurus"* is used by paleontologists to refer to this dinosaur.

The remains of approximately twenty individuals of *Apatosaurus* have been excavated from the Morrison Formation. Other remains identified as *Apatosaurus* have turned up in late Jurassic rocks of Portugal. In the Morrison Formation, *Apatosaurus* skeletons often have been found alone, not accompanied by other individuals of the same species, suggesting that *Apatosaurus* was less of a herd animal than *Camarasaurus* and *Diplodocus.*

Up until about 1910, when the partial skeleton of the huge *Brachiosaurus* was uncovered in Africa, *Apatosaurus* was considered the world's largest dinosaur. Our *Apatosaurus* skeleton stretches an impressive 76½ feet (23 m) in length and stands 14 feet 8 inches (4.5 m) at the hips. Yale's Peabody Museum has a slightly larger skeleton that stands 18 feet (5.5 m) at the hips.

Although *Apatosaurus* was slightly shorter than *Diplodocus,* it was much more heavily built. An adult *Apatosaurus* is estimated to have weighed up to 35 tons (32,000 kg), compared to the 12 tons (11,000 kg) of an adult *Diplodocus.*

Also compared to *Diplodocus, Apatosaurus'* neck vertebrae are wider. The projections running

parallel to the neck off the lower sides of each of *Apatosaurus'* vertebrae are actually fused ribs; they are exceptionally heavy in this sauropod. High spines on *Apatosaurus'* vertebrae between the hips and the shoulders, also present in *Diplodocus,* distinguish these genera from *Camarasaurus.* Like *Diplodocus, Apatosaurus* had a whiplash tail.

Despite its fame, for years paleontologists were not sure what an *Apatosaurus* skull looked like. Marsh first described *Apatosaurus ("Brontosaurus")* between 1877 and 1879. By 1883, feeling fairly certain he knew what the entire skeleton looked like, he put an artist to work drawing a reconstruction. For the missing head, Marsh arbitrarily selected a large skull collected 4 miles (6.4 km) from where the skeleton on which the reconstruction was based had been found. This skull could not be distinguished from that of an adult *Camarasaurus.* The image of *Apatosaurus* with a short-snouted, *Camarasaurus*-like head, therefore, quickly became entrenched in popular literature.

Not all dinosaur students were satisfied with the skull—especially because the *Apatosaurus* skeleton is much more like that of *Diplodocus* than that of *Camarasaurus.* The only evidence supporting Marsh's choice of a skull was a single *Camarasaurus*-like tooth found with the *Apatosaurus* skeleton exhibited at the American Museum of Natural History—a tooth that apparently was lost soon after it was unearthed.

When Earl Douglass discovered the quarry at Dinosaur National Monument in 1909, he began excavating a segment of an *Apatosaurus* tail exposed on the sandstone ledge. It turned out to be attached to one of the most complete skeletons of its kind thus far found. Almost the entire vertebral column, except for the very end of the tail, was found by Douglass. As usual, the skull was missing. About 12 feet (3.7 m) from the atlas vertebra, at the same level in the quarry, the field crew uncovered a detached sauropod skull that fit

*Skull of* Apatosaurus louisae *(C.M. Vertebrate Fossil No. 11162). Although discovered in 1909 along with the rest of this* Apatosaurus *skeleton, the skull was not exhibited with the rest of the skeleton until 1979. Research by John S. McIntosh and David S. Berman cleared up the controversy and mystery surrounding* Apatosaurus' *head.*

perfectly with the atlas. This skull was similar to that of *Diplodocus* but larger, in keeping with the robust build of *Apatosaurus*.

The Museum's *Apatosaurus* skeleton was prepared and mounted by 1915, in the record time of three years. At that time, Dr. W.J. Holland, Director of the Museum, announced the discovery of the skull to his fellow paleontologists, concluding that the long-missing head of *Apatosaurus* had finally been found. Several colleagues disagreed, however, and Holland never had the courage to install the skull on the newly mounted *Apatosaurus* skeleton. For more than twenty years the skeleton remained headless, awaiting the discovery of an *Apatosaurus* neck with the skull attached—a find still not made.

After Holland's death, a cast of an adult *Camarasaurus* skull was mounted with the *Apatosaurus* skeleton. It was not until 1936 that a monograph describing the dinosaur appeared. The work of C.W. Gilmore, the monograph reviewed the skull problem anew. In preparing the monograph, Gilmore had discussed the dilemma with J.L. Kay. Kay, who had worked for Douglass at the dinosaur quarry, had prepared a detailed diagram showing the exact location of every bone removed from the quarry and shipped to Pittsburgh. He informed Gilmore that Holland had been mistaken: The large, *Diplodocus*-like skull had come from the opposite side of the quarry and from a different level in the Morrison Formation than the rest of the *Apatosaurus* skeleton. The skull near the *Apatosaurus* was actually a large, *Camarasaurus*-like skull, explained Kay. Gilmore was not satisfied, however, and in his monograph concluded that the correct skull was still a mystery.

The matter of *Apatosaurus'* skull rested for more than thirty years. Then, another student of sauropods, John S. McIntosh, visited Carnegie Museum of Natural History and read the correspondence Holland had received from Douglass while the latter was directing the excavation at the dinosaur quarry. In the letter in which Douglass reported the finding of the *Diplodocus*-like skull near *Apatosaurus,* Douglass told Holland he believed the skull of *Apatosaurus* had finally been pinned down. McIntosh then discovered that an error in cataloging had apparently led Kay to conclude that Holland had been mistaken in attributing the *Diplodocus*-like skull to *Apatosaurus.* It seemed Holland had, in fact, been right all along.

October 20, 1979, was designated "Dinosaur Day" at Carnegie Museum of Natural History. On that date the *Camarasaurus* skull was replaced with the correct head. The celebration also commemorated th seventieth anniversary of the discovery of the *Apatosaurus* skeleton.

Although Carnegie Museum of Natural History has 69 catalogued specimens of *Apatosaurus,* most of them are single bones or only a few associated elements. Among these, Dr. McIntosh has identified the remains of four juveniles. The smallest *Apatosaurus,* represented by the shoulder, hip and limb bones and some fragmentary vertebrae, was found in a quarry at Sheep Creek, Wyoming, where the remains of an adult *Apatosaurus* were also found. Initially, the remains of the small *Apatosaurus* were described as a new kind of dinosaur, *Elosaurus parvus.* This little sauropod has an upper arm bone only 8¾ inches (22 cm), quite tiny compared to the 3 feet 9 inch (114 cm) upper arm bone of the Museum's mounted adult *Apatosaurus.* If all the bones of this little *Apatosaurus* were proportionately as small, the immature dinosaur would have been about 16 feet (5 m) long and 2 feet 10 inches (.86 m) high at the hips.

Three pieces of another juvenile *Apatosaurus* were found at Dinosaur National Monument. The three bones were closely associated with the adult *Apatosaurus* skeleton mounted in Dinosaur Hall. This second juvenile *Apatosaurus* was probably larger than *"Elosaurus."*

Dryosaurus altus *(C.M. Vertebrate Fossil No. 3392), a small, yet agile, ornithischian. This is the most complete* Dryosaurus *skeleton ever found. In life, this bipedal dinosaur probably could have outrun a predator such as* Allosaurus.

*Skull and neck vertebrae of* Dryosaurus altus *(C.M. Vertebrate Fossil No. 3392). This* Dryosaurus *skull is the only one known to date. An herbivore,* Dryosaurus *had jaws lined with teeth suitable for chewing vegetation; the front of the mouth was a horny beak. Although* Dryosaurus *probably had well-developed cheeks for holding food, its mouth is believed to have been small.*

# Jurassic Ornithischians

Three ornithischian ("bird-hipped") dinosaurs from the Jurassic Morrison Formation are displayed in Dinosaur Hall: *Dryosaurus, Camptosaurus,* and *Stegosaurus.*

### Dryosaurus

*Dryosaurus* was a small, plant-eating dinosaur. Its mounted skeleton measures 9 feet (2.7 m) long from the tip of its snout to the end of its tail and stands about 5 feet 10 inches (1.75 m) high. Collected at Dinosaur National Monument around 1922, it is the most complete *Dryosaurus* skeleton ever found. Though crushed, the *Dryosaurus* skull is the only one known. The *Dryosaurus* skeleton was put on display at Carnegie Museum of Natural History in 1940.

*Dryosaurus* is a hypsilophodontid. Of all of the ornithischian dinosaurs, the hypsilophodontids are among the closest to the dinosaurs' thecodont ancestors; they were small, agile, and bipedal. They do differ, however, in some important ways. As an ornithischian, *Dryosaurus* had the "bird-hipped" pelvis. Unlike the widely spaced, pointed teeth of its meat-eating ancestors, the teeth of *Dryosaurus* were designed to chew moderately tough plant material. Each tooth was elongated; the sides were strengthened by vertical ridges, and the cutting edges had coarse, saw-like serrations. There were no teeth at the front of its jaw which was covered by a horny sheath. The articulation of *Dryosaurus'* jaws permitted the teeth to come together simultaneously, increasing chewing efficiency.

*Dryosaurus* probably had well developed cheeks that permitted food to be held in its mouth while being chewed. The mouth itself was probably small, just as in modern herbivorous mammals such as deer, horses and cattle.

*Dryosaurus'* hands had five fingers, no doubt used for grasping objects. Its front legs were about half the length of the rear legs. *Dryosaurus* usually ran about on its sturdy hind legs, but sometimes dropped down on all fours, just as kangaroos do today. The three central toes bore the weight of the body. The first toe usually did not touch the ground, and the fifth toe was reduced to a single bone hidden in the flesh of the foot.

Ossified tendons, a series of thin, bony rods running along either side of the vertebral column from about the middle of the back to the front of the tail, stiffened the back and tail. When *Dryosaurus* ran, it lifted its tail well off the ground and probably held its body parallel to the ground.

*Dryosaurus,* as well as other hypsilophodontids, had large eyes reinforced by a ring of internal, over-lapping bony plates. Alert, small, lightweight, and fleet of foot, *Dryosaurus* was the equivalent of the deer and antelopes of today. An even better analogy is to the kangaroo, although dinosaur trackways demonstrate that hypsilophodontids ran rather than jumped. *Dryosaurus* and other dinosaurs in its family could easily outdistance ponderous *Allosaurus,* but the small, fast-running theropod predators were another matter.

The hypsilophodontid body plan was highly successful; this family survived the entire time span of the Age of the Reptiles with little change.

In addition to the *Dryosaurus* found in Dinosaur National Monument, its skeletal remains have been found in the famous East African late Jurassic deposits at Tendaguru, Tanzania. Other dinosaurs from the Morrison Formation of the western United States and from Tendaguru include *Brachiosaurus, Barosaurus,* and possibly *Allosaurus.* The similarity between the dinosaurs found in North America and Africa is evidence that these two continents were closer together during the Jurassic Period than in recent times.

*Camptosaurus medius (C.M. Vertebrate Fossil No. 11337), a plant-eating ornithischian of the Jurassic. Like its relative* Dryosaurus, *this bipedal dinosaur was a fairly swift runner. Ornithopods like* Camptosaurus *and* Dryosaurus *were the ancestors of many large herbivorous dinosaurs such as* Stegosaurus *and* Corythosaurus.

## Camptosaurus

*Camptosaurus* was a small- to medium-sized dinosaur, noteworthy as being near the ancestry of many other plant-eating dinosaurs. Although its descendants were generally larger and more specialized, *Camptosaurus* and its closer relatives went on their unassuming ways nearly to the end of the Mesozoic.

The earliest known and best preserved specimens of *Camptosaurus* come from the Morrison Formation. Hip bones belonging to a *Camptosaurus* have also been found in early Cretaceous deposits in South Dakota. Remains of *Camptosaurus* and its close relative *Rhabdodon* are also known from the middle and late Cretaceous in England, France, Spain, and Hungary.

Six species from the Morrison Formation of *Camptosaurus* have been named. These species range in size from the little *Camptosaurus nanus,* 6 feet (1.8 m) long, to *Camptosaurus dispar,* 20 feet (6 m) long. As its name implies, *Camptosaurus medius,* the species to which the skeleton in Dinosaur Hall is assigned, is medium-sized, about 15 feet (4.6 m) long and 10 feet (3 m) tall. There is some doubt as to whether Carnegie Museum of Natural History's *Camptosaurus* really represents a separate species; it might be a female or an immature *Camptosaurus dispar.* Not enough good *Camptosaurus* skeletons are available to determine this definitely.

Found at Dinosaur National Monument in 1922, Carnegie's *Camptosaurus* was put on exhibit in 1940. The skull, hind feet, and the end of the tail were restored from other specimens.

*Camptosaurus* had a small head that was carried on a gracefully curved neck of moderate length. There were no teeth at the front of its jaw; like *Dryosaurus, Camptosaurus* probably had a beak-like, horny sheath around its mouth. Single rows of teeth lined the rear portion of the upper and lower jaws. Individually rooted with serrations on the chewing edge, each tooth somewhat resembled a small, veined leaf. The abrasion of the plant material *Camptosaurus* ate wore down the serrations and much of the crown of the teeth. When a tooth became useless for chewing, it dropped out and was replaced by a new tooth growing from underneath. *Camptosaurus* thus enjoyed good teeth throughout its life.

Unlike many dinosaurs, *Camptosaurus* had five fingers. The three longest fingers had small, horny coverings resembling hooves. All four toes on the hind feet also had hooves. The inner hind toe was much smaller than the others and usually did not touch the ground when the animal walked.

*Camptosaurus'* front legs were half the length of its hind legs. When in a hurry this ornithischian probably ran on its hind legs and, often, such as when eating, dropped down on all four feet. *Camptosaurus* was a fairly swift runner, although perhaps not as speedy as *Dryosaurus.*

*Camptosaurus* occupies an important spot on the trunk of the ornithischian family tree. It is a descendant of the hypsilophodontids, the family to which *Dryosaurus* belongs. In turn, *Camptosaurus* and its family were the ancestors of many of the larger herbivorous dinosaurs of the late Jurassic and Cretaceous.

Some members of *Camptosaurus'* family developed long spines and upright plates along their backs; they lost the ability to walk solely on their hind legs. These herbivores were the ancestors of *Stegosaurus* and its relatives and of another branch, the armored dinosaurs.

Other members of *Camptosaurus'* family became quite dependent on their hind legs for walking and running. They also grew larger. Their toothless snouts became wide and flat, resembling the bill of a duck. The single row of teeth on each jaw multiplied into several rows packed tightly to form a single chewing surface that was extemely efficient in grinding up tough plant fibers. These members of the *Camptosaurus* family evolved into hadrosaurs—the duck-billed dinosaurs.

*Skull and neck vertebrae of* Camptosaurus medius *(C.M. Vertebrate Fossil No. 11337). This dinosaur had a good set of teeth throughout its life. As one of the teeth in the rear portion of* Camptosaurus' *jaw became worn and useless for chewing, it was replaced by a new tooth.*

Stegosaurus ungulatus *(C.M. Vertebrate Fossil No. 11341), an ornithischian of the Jurassic. One of the most bizarre dinosaurs,* Stegosaurus *had a small head with a walnut-sized brain and an arched body covered with bony plates and spikes. Although abundant and widespread in the late Jurassic,* Stegosaurus *appears to have declined rapidly at the end of that period.*

## Stegosaurus

*Stegosaurus* (Greek for "covered lizard") is the most bizarre dinosaur found in the Morrison Formation. *Stegosaurus* had a tiny head and small teeth with coarsely serrated edges. There were no teeth in the front of its mouth, which was probably sheathed with a horny, beak-like structure. *Stegosaurus* could probably chew only soft plant foods.

Although *Stegosaurus* walked on all four legs, its front legs were much shorter than the hind ones. As a result, its back arched over the hips, and its head was close to the ground. The legs were quite sturdy and its feet probably looked like those of an elephant or a large tortoise. The feet and the stout limbs were adapted for supporting its heavy body and armor plates. One dinosaur expert has maintained that *Stegosaurus* walked with a jolting, lumbering gait and was no more agile than a modern box turtle.

The spinal cord of *Stegosaurus* was enlarged in the hip region and occupied a large cavity. The enlargement was a bundle of nerve fibers running from the spinal cord to the heavy hind legs and tail. In almost all dinosaurs this enlargement was bigger than the brain. In the case of *Stegosaurus,* it was exceptionally so; its brain was very small—about one twentieth the size of the enlarged portion of the spinal cord.

Based on this description, *Stegosaurus* appears to have been an awkward, slow-moving,

rather defenseless creature—hardly a candidate for survival. Yet, not only did *Stegosaurus* outlive a number of other dinosaurs, but it was one of the more common North American dinosaurs of the late Jurassic.

*Stegosaurus* appears to be the last dinosaur in a particular lineage of ornithischians, the first ornithischian to diverge sharply from their small, bipedal ancestors. By the early Jurassic, stegosaurs had begun walking exclusively on all four feet. Some of the bony plates that serve as armor under the skin of many living and extinct reptiles were modified to spines. As the Jurassic Period progressed, the spines apparently enlarged and were restricted to one or two rows along the backbone. Those above the shoulders widened into plates. Eventually, all the spines, except those on the end of the tail, changed into plates. Some of the armor plates remained in the form of rounded, bony elements along the back and sides of the skeletons and across the back of the skulls.

*Stegosaurus'* most striking characteristics were the double row of alternating triangular plates located along the spine and upper part of the tail, and the four long spikes at the end of the tail. The plates were made of porous bone. Generally, they are restored standing upright, but some dinosaur specialists think they may have been movable and could be dropped down along the sides as well as raised erect.

The function of the bony plates and tail spikes is a mystery. One theory proposes that they defended the animals from predators such as *Allosaurus.* Could not *Allosaurus,* however, have attacked *Stegosaurus'* unprotected sides or bitten down between the plates? No doubt the tail spikes could inflict a nasty wound—if they hit the intended target. Tail spikes have been found broken, possibly suggesting that they were used for defense. One researcher, however, insists that because of the way the vertebrae fit together, the tail was stiff and inflexible and not particularly useful for protection.

Another theory maintains that the plates were mainly intended to impress other stegosaurs. Many modern animals have body structures, as well as modes of presenting themselves, to intimidate rivals or impress others of their own kind whether it be in rivalry for territory or mates or for wooing a member of the opposite sex. Several kinds of modern lizards, for example, present themselves broadside to rivals, flattening themselves from side to side to appear larger than they are. Perhaps *Stegosaurus* presented itself in a similar way. The effect of great size would have been emphasized if the plates could be raised suddenly or if they were brightly colored.

A third theory points to the plates as a means of regulating body temperature. Experiments conducted with a *Stegosaurus* model have indicated that the alternating arrangement of the plates, their shape, and the placement of the largest

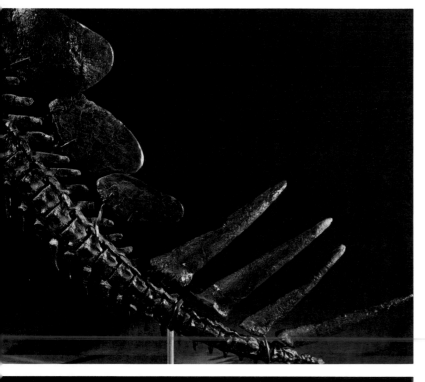

*Top: Tail of* Stegosaurus ungulatus *showing bony plates and spikes (C.M. Vertebrate Fossil No. 11341). Several theories have been proposed concerning the function of* Stegosaurus' *bony plates and tail spikes. One theory maintains that they helped this slow, lumbering dinosaur to defend itself from predators such as* Allosaurus. *Another holds that the plates, heavily profused with blood, served for thermoregulation.* **Bottom:** Stegosaurus ungulatus *(C.M. Vertebrate Fossil No. 11341) skull and neck vertebrae. Probably only soft plant food could be chewed by* Stegosaurus. *Its jaws were lined with small, coarsely serrated teeth. The tiny head ended in a toothless, horny, beak-like structure.*

plates at the highest point of the body appear to have been an effective means of dissipating heat. Both the surface and the interior of *Stegosaurus'* plates were richly supplied with blood vessels. By constricting and expanding the vessels and thus the amount of blood flowing through them, the dinosaur could increase or reduce heat loss. Other extinct reptiles such as *Edaphosaurus* and *Dimetrodon* from the Paleozoic Era, evolved upright fins thought to have functioned in this manner. Perhaps *Stegosaurus'* plates served all three purposes, or others no one has thought of yet.

Although stegosaurs were widespread and abundant in the late Jurassic, they seem to have declined rapidly at the end of that period. The last records of this dinosaur are from a few fragments found in lower Cretaceous deposits.

Possibly, *Allosaurus* and its kin proved too powerful for the stegosaurs in the long run. In addition, other plant-eating dinosaurs, including the armored dinosaurs (ankylosaurs) and the descendants of *Camptosaurus* may have crowded *Stegosaurus* out of its habitat. The teeth of these newer herbivores could handle tough plant fibers, while those of *Stegosaurus* restricted it to a diet of soft vegetation. These other herbivores were also better able to defend themselves and to flee from predators.

As an adult, *Stegosaurus* reached a length of 24 feet (7.3 m). The mounted skeleton in Dinosaur Hall, first exhibited in 1940, is 21 feet (6.4 m) long and 9½ feet (2.9 m) high at the hips. It is a composite based on a partial skeleton removed from the quarry at Dinosaur National Monument between 1920 and 1922 and the remains of other *Stegosaurus* skeletons found at the same quarry. The skull is a cast of a specimen at the Smithsonian Institution that was found at a quarry near Cañon City, Colorado.

# The Cretaceous Period

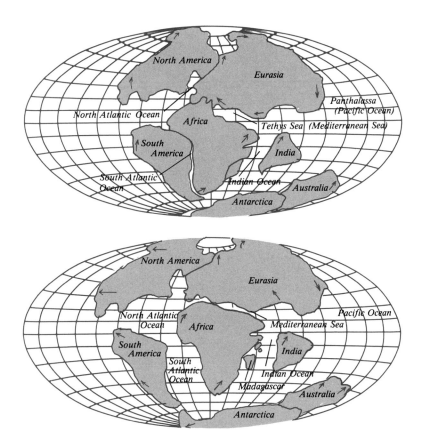

## Geography and Plant Life

The Cretaceous was the longest of the three periods of the Mesozoic Era, lasting approximately 78 million years. The Cretaceous ended with the mass extinction of many forms of life.

The name "Cretaceous" is derived from the Latin word "creta," meaning chalk. The name refers to the chalk deposits characteristic of this time period. The chalk is composed of the limy skeletons of microscopic marine organisms. In Europe, chalk deposits can be seen on both sides of the English Channel, including the famous White Cliffs of Dover. In North America, chalk deposits are prominent along the Gulf Coast and in the midwestern states.

The once-unified supercontinent Pangaea continued to split apart during the Cretaceous. By the end of the Mesozoic Era, South America had probably become a separate continent. North America and Eurasia were still connected at this time, while Eurasia and Africa remained separated by a narrow seaway. India was an island, drifting northward and destined eventually to collide with and join Asia.

Throughout the Cretaceous, large portions of the northern continental masses were covered by shallow seas; Europe was a mosaic of islands. After regressing during the late Jurassic, the seas invaded North America from the north and south through what is now the Rocky Mountain region. Seas also inundated the Gulf Coast. The northern and southern seas met during the late Cretaceous, splitting the North American land surface into two large islands. At the end of the Cretaceous, the seas began to regress, and rock layers began to be folded and thrust upward, initiating the building of the Rocky Mountains. What had formerly been a seaway gradually rose above sea level, giving way to swamps where extensive coal deposits formed.

*Top: At the beginning of the Cretaceous, the present-day continents of North America, Eurasia, South America, Africa, India, Antarctica and Australia continued to spread apart. The separation and drifting of the continental plates had initiated formation of the North and South Atlantic Oceans and the Indian Ocean. Arrows on the illustration indicate the direction of continental drift.* **Bottom:** *By the end of the Cretaceous, 65 million years ago, South America had become virtually isolated and Madagascar had split off from Africa, but Antarctica and Australia still remained attached. The Mediterranean Sea and the major oceans were evident. Approximately 15 million years later, India crashed into southern Asia, causing the rise of the Himalayan Mountains. Arrows on the illustration indicate the direction of continental drift. Both illustrations adapted from "The Break-Up of Pangaea" by Robert S. Dietz and John C. Holden. Copyright © 1970 by Scientific American, Inc. All rights reserved.*

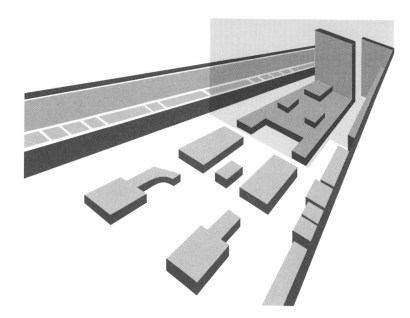

The Cretaceous, with a climate milder than that of today but perhaps not as warm as it had been during earlier times, was a crucial period in the history of land plants. At first, primitive types similar to those of the late Jurassic prevailed. Trees such as cypresses, araucarians, redwoods, and ginkgoes dotted the landscape, with cycads and various ferns forming the understory. The first evidence of angiosperms (flowering plants) is in the middle of the early Cretaceous. Gradually they became dominant. By the end of the Cretaceous, the flora of what is now Montana in the United States and Alberta in Canada was essentially modern, similar to that found today in Florida and along the Gulf Coast. Forests included oaks, magnolias, laurel, plane trees, and various tropical genera.

*Top: Cretaceous ammonite (C.M. Invertebrate Fossil No. 33642). Ammonites exhibited a great diversity of sizes and shapes during the Cretaceous Period.* ***Bottom:*** Pachydiscus coefeldensis *(C.M. Invertebrate Fossil No. 33060), a Cretaceous ammonite. Despite the diversity of sizes and shapes, an evolutionary adaptation to changing conditions, ammonites became extinct at the end of the Cretaceous.*

***Page 83:*** Baculites *sp. (C.M. Invertebrate Fossil No. 29829). This Cretaceous ammonite was almost straight, except for a coil that appeared at its oldest portion.*

# Invertebrates

## Ammonites

Ammonites reached their greatest diversity in the Cretaceous. Adults ranged in size from a fraction of an inch to more than 6 feet (2 m) in diameter. The largest ammonite on display in Carnegie Museum of Natural History's Dinosaur Hall is about 2 feet (60.9 cm) in diameter. Prior to the Cretaceous, as ammonites evolved, their suture patterns tended to become more complex. Some late Cretaceous ammonites reversed this trend and developed relatively simple sutures.

Although Triassic ammonites had coiled shells, some late Cretaceous ammonites, such as *Baculites* in Dinosaur Hall, developed straight shells similar to its relatives of the Paleozoic Era. Some such as *Ancyloceras* and *Cirroceras* developed loose spirals so that the coils did not touch each other. Others coiled when they were young, then straightened out. As shown by the four examples in Dinosaur Hall, *Scaphites,* during its lifetime, first coiled in one direction, then straightened out in mid-section, and finally coiled in the reverse direction. *Turrilites,* also on exhibit in Dinosaur Hall, developed a high, conical shell amazingly similar to that of *Turritella,* a snail common in the Tertiary Period of the Cenozoic Era. *Emperoceras* had its loose coils piled one atop the other like a coiled snake. Still other ammonites grew in U-shapes.

In their varied forms, ammonites almost certainly had different habits and habitats. The compressed, smooth-shelled ammonites such as *Planticeras* and *Desmoceras bendanti* were probably fast swimmers. Irregularly coiled types such as *Cirroceras* and *Turrilites* may have been bottom dwellers. Still others such as *Scaphites* and *Heteroceras,* which grew in a snail-like coil when young and a wide curve when older, may have had different habits at different stages of their lives.

Because of their rapid evolution, great diversity, widespread geographic distribution, and easy means of identification, ammonites are among the most useful organisms employed in dating sedimentary rocks.

After existing for more than 340 million years, the ammonites became extinct at the end of the Cretaceous Period. Their close relatives, the nautiloids, persisted to the present day.

## Bivalves

Clams and other kinds of bivalve molluscs flourished during the Cretaceous. Bivalves (often termed pelecypods in scientific literature) are protected by two symmetrical shells called valves. The valve on the left side of the body is joined to the valve on the right side of the body at a flexible hinge line that extends over the back of the animal. One or two powerful muscles act to pull the valves closed. When the muscles relax, ligaments in the hinge automatically pull the valves apart.

Some adult bivalves can pull themselves slowly along the ocean floor. Their single, muscular foot protrudes from between the lower front of the valves, as it grasps the substrate, the animal is pulled forward.

Bivalves start life as free-swimming larvae but eventually settle down on the bottom of the ocean floor. Although a few adult bivalves, such as the scallop, can swim by clapping their shells together, most species cannot. Many bivalves firmly attach themselves to rock and other solid objects by thread-like, horny secretions that are exuded from the foot. *Inoceramus* was one Cretaceous bivalve that attached itself to the bottom in this manner. Large and small examples of *Inoceramus,* an important mollusc when identifying Cretaceous deposits, can be seen in Dinosaur Hall.

Like other bivalves, young oysters go through a free-swimming larval stage. Known as spat, the young, mobile oysters grow two symmetrical, smooth valves. Soon, however, the left valve grows larger than the right. The spat settles to the bottom on some hard object, lying on its left valve. A secretion from the foot is used to cement the spat to the object. The left valve continues to grow larger, while the right valve is modified into a kind of lid. An oyster conforms to some extent to the shape of the substrate and, thus, may be irregular in form.

Two members of the family Ostreidae are among the Cretaceous oysters exhibited. Known

*Top: Cretaceous ammonite (C.M. Invertebrate Fossil No. 33643). While some ammonites were no bigger than marbles, others were 7 feet in diameter. **Bottom left:** Cirroceras sp. (C.M. Invertebrate Fossil Nos. 7637 and 29908), ammonite found in late Cretaceous deposits of South Dakota. The coils of some Cretaceous ammonites such as Cirroceras developed into loose spirals. **Bottom right:** Turrilites sp. (C.M. Invertebrate Fossil No. 7635), a Cretaceous ammonite found in France. Unlike the normal, tightly coiled forms, many Cretaceous ammonites developed unusual shapes. The high, conical shape of Turrilites is similar to that of a snail common during the Tertiary Period of the Cenozoic Era. Like a snail, Turrilites spent a great deal of time on the ocean bottom.*

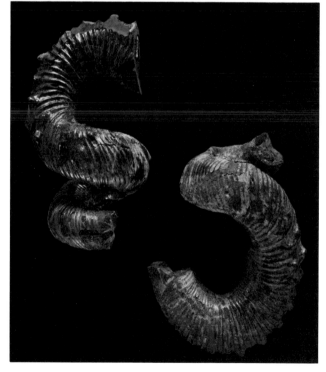

*Left:* Placenticeras *sp. (C.M. Invertebrate Fossil No. 29854), an ammonite from the late Cretaceous deposits of South Dakota. Its compressed, smooth shell suggests that it was a fast swimmer. Teeth marks found on some* Placenticeras *fossils indicate that these ammonites occasionally were fed on by mosasaurs.* **Below:** *Ancyloceras gigas (C.M. Invertebrate Fossil No. 25568), a Cretaceous ammonite. During the Cretaceous, ammonites reached their greatest diversity. Some, such as* Ancyloceras, *developed loose spirals.*

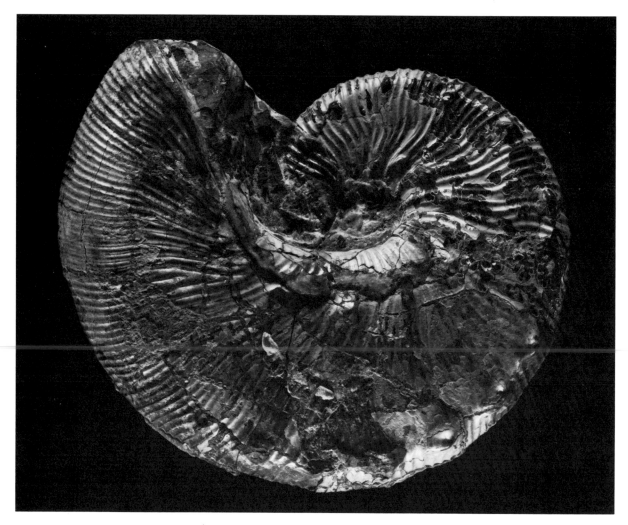

*Above:* Scaphites *sp. (C.M. Invertebrate Fossil No. 29891), a late Cretaceous ammonite found in South Dakota. The tightly coiled center represents the young* Scaphites. *As it grew older, the coils became wider. Perhaps the different shapes represent adaptations to differing environmental conditions throughout various stages of its life.* **Left:** Hippurites *sp. (C.M. Invertebrate Fossil No. 1101), a clam found in Cretaceous deposits in France. Only known in the Cretaceous, fossils of this huge, modified clam are found in the chalks and limestone of the English Channel region.* Hippurites *lived in groups on reefs or attached to the ocean bottom. Its one shell was reduced to a lid while the other formed an elongated, thick-shelled cone.*

as the true oysters, members of this group are now raised commercially.

Today's descendants of the deeply fluted *Lopha diluviana* and *Lopha* sp. live in tropical waters. Note the claspers growing from the ribs, with which *Lopha* grasped the shell or other object on which it grew.

Oysters in the family Gryphaeidae reached their peak during the Cretaceous and have only two descendants living today. Several members of this group had spirally coiled lower valves with a small attachment area at the tip of the coil. In contrast to the true oysters, this family was generally adapted for life in deeper waters with a softer, muddier bottom. Nonetheless, like the true oysters, most had to find at least a small shell fragment or other solid object in order to attach itself initially. Once a gryphaeid spat found such an object, it attached itself, and the lower valve began to grow straight upward. Eventually, the shell toppled over in the mud, but it continued to grow upward with the right valve (or lid) uppermost. Repeated falls produced a lower valve with an angular outline on the bottom, while gradual slumps produced a lower valve with a smooth curve. Despite the repeated falls, the upper valve always remained on top, out of the mud.

One Cretaceous member of this family, *Exogyra costata,* had upper and lower valves that grew in a spiral. A spat of this type attached itself to an object on the ocean bottom by the rear margin of its left valve. The unattached front margin grew faster than the attached rear margin, producing a spiral pattern. Three examples of *Exogyra costata* can be located in Dinosaur Hall, as can another member of the family Gryphaeidae, *Pycnodonte convexa*. Although both of these species of Cretaceous oysters are extinct today, the genus *Pycnodonte* survived until the middle of the Cenozoic Era.

Early paleontologists had trouble deciding what the rudists were. They resembled oysters in that one valve, although not necessarily the left, was usually cemented to the substrate. There is, however, no other evidence that they are closely related.

In some rudists both valves were coiled, but in different planes. *Requienia,* a rudist displayed in Dinosaur Hall and known to have lived in

groups on reefs, was fastened by the tip of its spirally, whorled valve while the "lid" grew in a flat whorl. Other rudists were attached by the tip of a cone-shaped valve resembling the horn corals of the Paleozoic Era. Externally, the upper valve resembled a pot lid, but underneath, two huge hinge teeth and a socket meshed with a corresponding tooth and socket in the attached valve. This arrangement allowed the lid to move up and down without coming off. Some rudists of this type—*Radiolites mammilaris, Radiolites bournoni,* and *Hippurites*—are displayed in Dinosaur Hall. The name *"Hippurites"* means "horsetail" and refers to the overall shape of the shell.

Rudists lived mainly in shallow seas near the equator, especially in the vast Tethys seaway that once extended from present-day Mexico through the Caribbean Sea and across what is now the Mediterranean Sea, the Alps, and the Himalayas. Some rudists were solitary, but others were gregarious and formed low reefs associated with sponges and other animals but not with corals. Apparently, rudists and the scleractinian corals, which formed huge reefs, could not co-exist.

During the late Cretaceous, the huge coral reefs were supplanted by low rudist reefs in equatorial areas. With the extinction of the rudists, coral reefs reappeared in the lower latitudes.

Rudists first appeared in the late Jurassic and became numerous and diverse during the Cretaceous; then they abruptly disappeared. Their demise is one of the many mysteries of the end of the Cretaceous.

# Fishes

Bony fish underwent great changes during the Cretaceous. Early in this period, primitive forms of bony fish, represented today by the gars and bowfin, predominated. By the late Cretaceous, the ancestors of the teleost fish had become dominant in both salt and fresh waters. Most modern fish are teleosts, descendants of *Leptolepis* of the late Jurassic or of something similar to it. In comparison to its antecedents, *Leptolepis* had developed a highly mobile mouth that was more

*Left:* Sardinoides *sp. (C.M. Vertebrate Fossil No. 5182), a bony fish from the late Cretaceous deposits of Germany. Related to the living lantern fish,* Sardinoides *had a spiny ray at the front of its dorsal fin. The small fish seen with* Sardinoides *is a true herring.*

*Below: Three late Cretaceous predaceous fish.* Istieus gracilis *(C.M. Vertebrate Fossil No. 25464) (top), found in Cretaceous deposits in Germany. This predator had a long dorsal fin for maneuvering slowly among water plants.* Eurypholis boissieri *(C.M. Vertebrate Fossil No. 4644) (bottom left), found in Syria. This powerful predator is related to the modern lantern fish.* Spaniodon blondelli *(C.M. Vertebrate Fossil No. 5196) (bottom right), found in Cretaceous sediments in Syria. This was a small, fast-swimming predator related to the living ten-pounder, a South Atlantic and Caribbean game fish.*

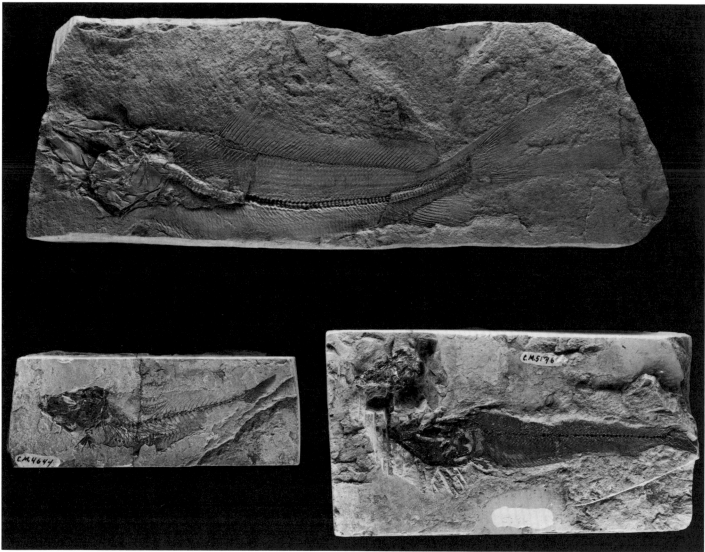

effective in feeding. In the Cretaceous its descendants added refinements in their swimming ability. The enamel-like layer of ganoine disappeared from their scales, and their backs were strengthened by the development of bony vertebrae and specialized tailbones.

Dinosaur Hall features late Cretaceous fish found in several localities in England, Germany, Lebanon, Syria, and the United States. *Diplomystus brevissimus,* a herring and close relative of the shad, is among the specimens on exhibit.

*Diplomystus,* like *Leptolepis,* had a mouth that allowed it to feed on plankton. Now extinct, *Diplomystus* survived into the Eocene Epoch of the Cenozoic. It is common in the famous Eocene Green River shales of Wyoming.

Even before the Jurassic ended, *Thrissops,* a predaceous fish, had evolved from *Leptolepis.* Modern relatives of *Thrissops,* such as the tarpon, have changed little from their forebears of the Cretaceous. Four fish related to *Thrissops* and the tarpons are displayed in Dinosaur Hall. Gigantic *Xiphactinus* and its smaller relative *Ichthyodectes* swam the shallow sea that once extended across western Kansas. *Spaniodon blondelli* was a small, fast swimmer related to the modern ten-pounder or ladyfish, a game fish of South Atlantic and Caribbean waters. *Istieus gracilis* had a long dorsal fin similar to that of modern fish that move slowly backward or forward among water plants by rippling their long dorsal fins.

*Sardinoides, Eurypholis,* and *Cassandra* are related to the present-day lantern fish, so-called because they have rows of luminous light-producing organs along their sides. Some modern lantern fish avoid light, sinking to depths of 500 feet (152 m) during the day and rising to the surface of the ocean at night. *Sardinoides,* with its spiny rays in the front of its dorsal fin, was more advanced than the earlier herrings and tarpon-like fish. *Eurypholis,* a predator armed with powerful teeth and a protective row of large scales along its back, was an excellent swimmer.

A slab of limestone found in Syria is completely covered with juvenile *Cassandra minimus* about 1¼ inches (3.2 cm) long. This slab of limestone is an example of a "fish-kill layer," the remnant of some marine catastrophe. Some scientists speculate that the fish kill was brought on by

something similar to the modern "Red Tide," blooms of red marine algae that secrete lethal toxins causing massive fish kills.

A collection of scales in Dinosaur Hall belongs to *Lepisosteus,* the gar. The approximately ½ inch (1.3 cm) long scales of *Lepisosteus* were found in Cretaceous deposits in northwestern Montana. Each scale had a thick, bony base that appears gray in the fossils as well as an outer layer of shiny, black ganoine. This kind of scale was typical of the gar-like fish dominant during the Jurassic and Triassic. True gars, however, were not present until the late Cretaceous. Today, *Lepisosteus* is still found in fresh and brackish waters.

Most modern sharks and the predecessors of living skates and rays were present by the late Cretaceous. A piece of sandstone from the Netherlands in Dinosaur Hall has several shark teeth embedded in it. Shark teeth from the Cretaceous are also common in marine deposits along the east coast of North America from central New Jersey south into South Carolina.

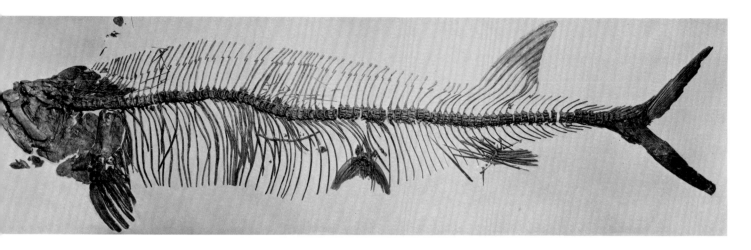

*Above:* Xiphactinus molossus *(C.M. Vertebrate Fossil No. 4101 and 4102), a gigantic, predaceous bony fish from the late Cretaceous deposits of western Kansas. It is related to the Jurassic fish* Thrissops. *Left:* Protostega gigas *(C.M. Vertebrate Fossil No. 1420), a late Cretaceous marine turtle found in the Niobrara Chalk of western Kansas. The strong, flipper-like limbs suggest that* Protostega *was a powerful swimmer. It probably depended on speed rather than armor to protect itself from predators also living in the seas then covering western North America.*

# Vertebrates from Kansas' Niobrara Sea

Many of the Cretaceous vertebrates in Dinosaur hall come from exposures of the Niobrara Chalk on the Smoky Hill drainage in western Kansas. This formation contains an excellent record of life about 79 million years ago in the shallow Niobrara Sea.

Fish from the Niobrara Sea are well represented in Dinosaur Hall. *Xiphactinus* is the largest known teleost that ever lived. The Museum's specimen measures 14 feet 10 inches (4.45 m) long; thus far, the largest collected has been 16 feet (4.9 m) long. *Xiphactinus* used its long, pointed teeth for seizing other fish. The skeleton of the largest known *Xiphactinus* contains the complete skeleton of another fish, *Ichthyodectes,* that had been swallowed head first. Fragmentary remains of *Ichthyodectes* have also been found inside other skeletons of *Xiphactinus*

*Xiphactinus* was collected by Charles Sternberg and was prepared and put on exhibit in 1910 by Arthus S. Coggeshall. The last eleven vertebrae and the tail come from another specimen also collected by Sternberg.

Several kinds of marine turtles adapted for life in the open seas appear in the late Cretaceous. Some were very large. The *Protostega gigas* skeleton on exhibit has a 3 foot 11 inch (1.17 m) long shell. It was the cousin of a living marine turtle also first known from late Cretaceous deposits. Although *Protostega* survived the great extinctions at the end of the Mesozoic Era, it is not known to have existed after the middle of the Cenozoic Era.

The shell of *Protostega* consisted of a lattice of bone, not a solid, bony carapace, an obvious weight-reducing adaptation. *Protostega* and its relatives also lost the ability to withdraw their heads, legs, and tails into the shells. Their forelegs became paddles for rowing their huge bodies through the water. *Protostega* probably preyed on free-swimming animals, as do today's leatherback and loggerhead turtles.

The Museum's mounted *Protostega* skeleton is a composite incorporating portions of at least two partial skeletons. Collected by Charles Sternberg in 1903 and 1905, the mount was prepared by Louis and Arthur Coggeshall and placed on exhibit in 1911.

Mosasaurs, huge marine reptiles of the late Cretaceous, are more abundant and diverse in the Niobrara Chalk than in any other formation on earth. A 15 foot (4.5 m) long skeleton of *Clidastes* from the chalk is mounted on the wall in Dinosaur Hall along with a free-mounted 21 foot (6.3 m) *Mosasaurus* skeleton from Belgium. Some mosasaurs reached a length of 60 feet (18 m).

The nostrils of mosasaurs were near the top of the head. Other unrelated, air-breathing vertebrates have also developed this feature that permits them to breathe with only the tops of the heads remaining out of the water. They had keen eyesight and excellent hearing but a poor sense of smell.

Mosasaurs had paddle-like feet and tails that were compressed from side to side. *Clidastes* and *Mosasaurus* had low fins on top of their tail. They swam by undulating their bodies and tails from side to side, steering and balancing with their paddles.

Mosasaurs had conical heads and elongated bodies. Their jaws were armed with pointed teeth. Their lower jaws were hinged in the middle, and the bones of the cranium were not rigidly attached to one another. This jaw arrangement allowed mosasaurs to dismember and swallow large prey.

This was helpful since a typical mosasaur was a voracious predator that fed on free-swimming animals—predominantly medium-sized fish. Also included in their diet were ammonites, squids, sea-turtles, and, occasionally a juvenile mosasaur. Some mosasaur skeletons show evidence of severe wounds apparently inflicted by other mosasaurs. One mosasaur, *Globidens,* had almost spherical teeth, presumably for cracking the shells of bottom-dwelling molluscs.

Remains of juvenile mosasaurs are rare. The youngest known is a 4 foot (1.2 m) long *Clidastes* found in the Niobrara Chalk deposits. Adult skeletons provide no evidence that mosasaurs bore their young alive like ichthyosaurs. Perhaps gravid females swam up large rivers and climbed ashore to lay and bury their eggs on the banks.

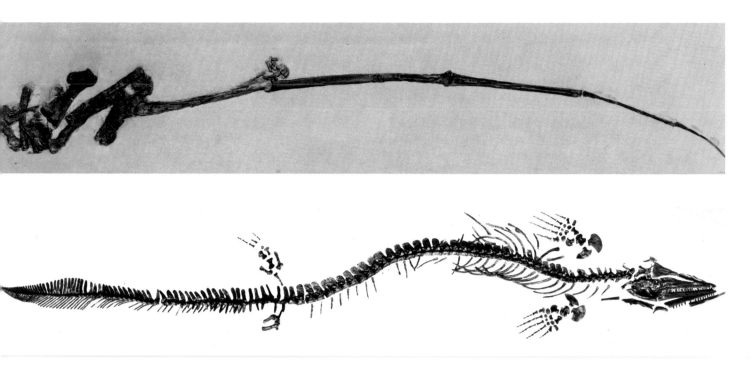

Mosasaurs were almost certainly related to the monitor lizards. During the early part of the late Cretaceous, two lineages of monitor-like lizards became semi-aquatic. One of these lines evolved into mosasaurs. The largest living lizard, the Komodo dragon of the East Indies, is a monitor. It reaches a length of 10 or 12 feet (approximately 3.4 m). Some mosasaurs were as much as 60 feet (18 m) long.

The skeleton of the mosasaur *Clidastes propython* on display in Dinosaur Hall is a composite of at least two partial skeletons from Logan County, Kansas. One of these skeletons, collected by Charles H. Sternberg in 1904, included the skull, front paddles, neck vertebrae, and two vertebrae from the back. The other, collected by C.W. Gilmore in 1903, accounts for additional vertebrae as far back as the middle of the tail. The end of the tail and the rear paddles come from other partial skeletons.

The skeleton of *Mosasaurus lemonnieri* is a composite of two specimens from Cueames, Belgium. Paddles were missing from both specimens. *Mosasaurus* is not common in the Niobrara Chalk but has been found in late Cretaceous deposits at many localities in North America and Europe. Although it was similar to *Clidastes,* it averages somewhat larger and heavier.

No remains of the porpoise-like ichthyosaurs have turned up in the Niobrara Chalk. They are uncommon in deposits dating from the early part of the late Cretaceous, and only a single bone has been identified from the later part of the Cretaceous. As the ichthyosaurs died out, the mosasaurs apparently took over their niches in the seas.

Both the small-headed and long-necked as well as the large-headed and short-necked plesiosaurs have been found in the Niobrara Chalk deposits. They, along with the mosasaurs, flourished up to the time of the great extinctions at the end of the Cretaceous.

At least two kinds of pterosaurs soared over the Niobrara Sea. Both "winged reptiles," the large *Nyctosaurus* and the gigantic *Pteranodon,* are displayed in Dinosaur Hall. They were collected by H.T. Martin in 1920. Like *Pterodactylus* (also in Dinosuar Hall) of the late Jurassic Solnhofen deposits, both *Nyctosaurus* and *Pteranodon* were short-tailed. Long-tailed pterosaurs such as *Campylognathoides* and *Rhamphorhynchus* had become extinct at the end of the Jurassic Period.

*Nyctosaurus* had a wingspread of up to 7 or 8 feet (2.3 m). with its long, toothless beak, *Nyctosaurus* probably consumed fish, perhaps a little like the modern-day tern.

*Pteranodon* is represented in Dinosaur Hall by a portion of a wing. Note that the crushed bones are very thin-walled. In life, the bones of pterosaurs were filled with air sacs. *Pteranodon* had an estimated wingspan of up to 22 feet (6.7 m).

*Pteranodon* had a huge, toothless beak counterbalanced by a long, bony crest at the back of the skull. It was equipped with a pelican-like pouch; remains of fish have been found in the impression of one known *Pteranodon* pouch. *Pteranodon* may have fished "on the wing," gliding just over the surface of the water and dipping its beak to pluck out fish. The vertebrae of the neck were capable of little side-to-side motion, but the neck could be curved up into a vertical S-shape permitting the beak to strike with great force.

*Pteranodon* was perhaps closest to the modern albatross in appearance and habits. It may have been capable of little flapping flight but no doubt was a superb glider, spending hours or even days gliding on uplifting air currents. Remains of *Pteranodon* found in the Niobrara Chalk deposits occur at sites that were at least 99 miles (160 km) from the nearest shore.

Until recently, most students of pterosaurs assumed that *Pteranodon* must have had difficulty becoming airborne. They speculated that it had to launch itself from cliffs or treetops. If pterosaurs were bipedal, however, *Pteranodon* may have taken off merely by facing into the wind, flapping its wings, and kicking off with its legs.

There has also been some speculation regarding the function of the head crest. While in some *Pteranodon* specimens the long crest doubles the length of the skull, *Nyctosaurus* had only a rudimentary crest. Other large pterosaurs, including perhaps some *Pteranodon* specimens, had none. If these pteranodons really were crestless in life, then the crests were probably most important in communicating with others of their own species. Either males or females could have had crests to attract the opposite sex or for display in disputes over territory or mates.

Until a few years ago, *Pteranodon* was the largest known flying creature. In 1975, a new genus of pterosaur, *Quetzalcoatlus,* was discovered in late Cretaceous deposits at Big Bend National Park, Texas. The largest specimen was a partial wing from an individual with an estimated wing span of 36 or 39 feet (11 or 12 m). Scattered bones of at least twelve similar but smaller pterosaurs were found at other localities in the park. *Quetzalcoatlus* appears to have been associated with a terrestrial fauna, including sauropod dinosaurs. Perhaps it fed on dead dinosaurs, much as condors once scavenged the carcasses of the giant mammals of the Ice Age. Or, it may have walked over periodically flooded mud flats probing for molluscs and arthropods, as do shore birds today.

Pterosaurs apparently were not as diverse in the late Cretaceous as they had been earlier in the Mesozoic. Perhaps they were competitively edged out by the birds.

Although neither is displayed in Dinosaur Hall, the Niobrara Chalk is noted for two kinds of fossil sea birds: *Hesperornis* and *Ichthyornis. Hesperornis* was a diving bird that looked somewhat like a loon. Its legs were set far back on its body, making it a proficient swimmer and diver but hampering its ability to walk. The wings had degenerated, leaving *Hesperornis* flightless. Unlike all modern birds, it had teeth.

*Ichthyornis* stood about 8 inches (20 cm) high. It was a good flyer and probably resembled a gull or tern. Like *Hesperornis, Ichthyornis* was a toothed bird.

Fragmentary remains of birds assigned to five orders of living birds—including loons, grebes, pelicans, herons, and gulls—have been found in

*Left: Skull of* Protoceratops andrewsi *(C.M. Vertebrate Fossil No. 9185). A prominent frill extended from the back of* Protoceratops' *disproportionately large skull. In life, the large openings in the frill were covered with skin. A hooked beak formed the front of* Protoceratops' *mouth, whereas leaf-shaped teeth grew in a single row farther back on each jaw.* **Below:** Protoceratops andrewsi *(C.M. Vertebrate Fossil No. 9185), a ceratopsian dinosaur, was a small quadrupedal herbivore. This partly grown* Protoceratops *was among over one hundred found in the Djadochta Formation of the Mongolian People's Republic. As depicted in Dinosaur Hall, many egg clutches have been found associated with* Protoceratops *skeletons.*

deposits from the late Cretaceous. It is not surprising that most of the birds found are water birds, since most of the fossilized remains were found in marine deposits. Inland types of birds almost certainly existed in the late Cretaceous, but their fragile remains are rarely preserved.

# Terrestrial Reptiles of the Late Cretaceous

The late Cretaceous covers the last fifteen million years of the Mesozoic Era. This interval brought the Age of Reptiles to a close. At its end, massive extinctions occurred.

The four late Cretaceous dinosaurs in Dinosaur Hall were found in such widespread areas as Mongolia in central Asia and Montana in the western United States. During the late Cretaceous, North America and Eurasia were still connected across the North Atlantic and interchange of dinosaurs may have occurred.

## *Protoceratops*

At roughly the same time mosasaurs and giant marine turtles swam over western Kansas, *Protoceratops* thrived in what is now the desert of Mongolia. At the time this small, quadrupedal dinosaur lived, geologists believe the region was semi-arid and dotted with fresh water lakes.

More than one hundred *Protoceratops* specimens have been collected from the Djadochta Formation at the base of the Flaming Cliffs in Mongolia. The remains of very young animals as well as adults have been found along with nests of eggs containing the remnants of *Protoceratops* embryos.

*Protoceratops* was a small dinosaur; although adults sometimes reached a length of 8 feet (2.4 m), more commonly they were 5 or 6 feet (1.5 m) long. The skull of *Protoceratops* was disproportionately large, and a frill covered the back of its neck. The large openings apparent in the bones of the frill were covered with skin in life.

*Protoceratops* had a hooked beak. The front of the beak was toothless, whereas leaf-shaped

teeth grew in a single row farther back in each jaw. The upper teeth met the lower ones in an oblique plane. As in all dinosaurs, worn-out teeth were continuously replaced by new ones growing beneath the bone.

From specimens found thus far, two types of *Protoceratops* skulls are distinguishable: One type has a bump on the snout that, in life, apparently supported a rudimentary horn. This type of skull is more robust and has a wider frill at the back of the neck. The other type of *Protoceratops* skull is narrower and more delicately built and, though almost as large as the first type, has no bump. The difference between the two skull types is less pronounced in smaller individuals that are presumably younger. The robust skulls may be those of males while the more delicately built skulls may belong to females.

The frill may have served to impress and intimidate other *Protoceratops* as well as to protect the dinosaur against predators. Perhaps rivals stood face to face shaking their heads to show off their wide frills. Contestants also may have pushed and shoved each other with their little horns.

Many eggs have been found associated with *Protoceratops* skeletons. The clutches, laid in concentric circles, contained twelve, fifteen or more elongated eggs, each egg being about 8 inches (20 cm) long and having a rough surface. In life, the shell was probably leathery, as it is in modern reptiles. Evidently, a female *Protoceratops* dug a hole in the sand for her eggs and then covered them, allowing the sun's warmth to provide for incubation. Although probable dinosaur eggs have been discovered in other rock formations, the Djadochta is among the few in which the eggs and the egg-layers are almost certainly associated.

*Protoceratops* is one of the earliest ceratopsians or horned dinosaurs. This group is known only in the late Cretaceous and flourished in Asia and western North America up to the end of the Mesozoic. During this time, the ceratopsians and the hadrosaurs were the most abundant dinosaurs.

According to recent studies, the horned dinosaurs evolved during the Cretaceous from the family Hypsilophodontidae of which *Dryosaurus* was a member. The family Protoceratopidae, to which *Protoceratops* belongs, included small

Corythosaurus casuarius *(C.M. Vertebrate Fossil No. 9461 and cast of R.O.M. 5856) from late Cretaceous deposits in Dinosaur Provincial Park, near Steveville, Alberta (Canada). This and other duck-billed dinosaurs were herbivorous and semi-aquatic. They had webbed feet, a laterally compressed tail, and a duck-like bill. Some, like* Corythosaurus, *had a bony crest on top of the skull.*

dinosaurs from both Asia and North America. Unlike the larger ceratopsids within the suborder of ceratopsians, protoceratopsids never had horns above their eyes, but some had single horns on their snouts. (See "Scientific Names" in Appendix.)

The *Protoceratops* skeleton displayed in Dinosaur Hall was collected by the American Museum of Natural History in 1925. Shown with it is a cast of a partial clutch of eggs. The mounted skeleton, measuring about 51 inches (130 cm) long and 20 inches (51 cm) high, is from a partly grown animal, possibly a male. Serafino Agostino mounted the skeleton which was first put on display in 1945 or 1946 and then removed and redisplayed in 1979.

### Corythosaurus

About 76 million years ago, a floodplain with great expanses of cat-tail marsh spread along the western edge of the sea that bisected North America from north to south. On the better-drained ground, semi-tropical forests grew. Here—in what is now the southern portion of the Canadian province of Alberta and the western portion of the state of Montana—dawn redwoods, sycamores, yews, katsura trees, lycopods (ground pines), and ferns flourished. During periodic floods, the rivers deposited sands and clays on the plain. Known today as the Oldman Formation, these deposits have preserved an excellent sample of dinosaur life in this region during the late Cretaceous.

Although the Morrison Formation of late Jurassic age contains some spectacular mass assemblages of dinosaur bones, the Oldman Formation has produced more individual dinosaur specimens and more species than any other geological formation in the world. A portion of the most productive area, designated Dinosaur Provincial Park, is located about 120 miles (185 km) southwest of Calgary, Alberta.

Among the inhabitants of the late Cretaceous floodplain now called the Oldman Formation were turtles, crocodilians, champsosaurs, small mammals, and true lizards. Small and large carnivorous theropod dinosaurs roamed the plains. Smaller theropods including the dromaeosaurids and struthiomimids were quite active. The dromaeosaurids, about the size of a human and weighing 100 to 200 pounds (45 to 90 kg), had long-fingered hands for grasping prey and a large, curved, extra-sharp claw on the inner toe of each hind foot. The struthiomimids, or ostrich dinosaurs, had small heads, long necks, and long tails.

At least two genera of large theropods, *Albertosaurus* and *Daspletosaurus,* preyed on the larger herbivores of the time. Both are classified in the same family as *Tyrannosaurus*—which had not yet appeared on the scene. *Albertosaurus,* also known as *Gorgosaurus,* reached a length of 25 feet (7.6 m), somewhat smaller than *Tyrannosaurus* but still impressive.

The large, plant-eating sauropods such as *Diplodocus,* so common in the Morrison Formation, have not been found in the Oldman Forma-

tion. Instead, the Oldman herbivores consisted of three types: armored dinosaurs, horned dinosaurs (ceratopsians), and hadrosaurs. At least three kinds of horned dinosaurs lived on the plain, although *Triceratops* had not yet evolved.

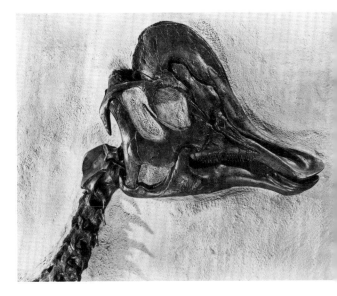

Corythosaurus casuarius *(C.M. Vertebrate Fossil No. 9461 and skull cast from R.O.M. 5856). The hollow, semi-circular crest atop this duck-billed dinosaur's skull reminded its discoverer of the helmets worn by Corinthian warriors of ancient Greece. Small, tightly packed teeth lined the back portion of* Corythosaurus' *jaw. They were used to grind up tough plant material.*

Hadrosaurs, the most abundant dinosaurs found in the Oldman Formation, were flat-snouted ornithischians that walked on their hind legs, although they probably dropped down on all fours when moving slowly. Carbonaceous remains and impressions show that, in life, the fronts of their jaws were sheathed in a horny, squared-off beak; their common name, duckbilled dinosaur, is derived from the shape of their jaws. Three general types of hadrosaurs are known: those with relatively small, solid crests or spikes projecting from their foreheads or back from between their eyes; those with much larger, at least partially hollow crests; and those usually without a crest.

*Corythosaurus,* the most abundant hadrosaur found in the Oldman Formation, is one of the hollow-crested hadrosaurs. Its semi-circular crest reminded its discoverer of the helmets worn by the Corinthian warriors of ancient Greece; thus, its name was coined.

In comparison to other specimens of Corythosaurus, Carnegie Museum's is small. One complete skeleton, for example, is 31 feet (9.5 m) long, more than twice the size of that on display in Dinosaur Hall. Carnegie Museum's skeleton, obtained from the Royal Ontario Museum in Toronto in 1940, was collected by Levi Sternberg southeast of Steveville, Alberta, in 1920. The skull, jaws, tip of the tail, one lower arm bone, and both hands, missing from the original find, were replaced by casts of the appropriate parts from other specimens. The completed *Corythosaurus* was put on exhibit in Dinosaur Hall in 1941.

At least one complete mummified *Corythosaurus* has been found along with others with skin impressions from various parts of the body. As a result, scientists have an excellent idea of what a living *Corythosaurus* looked like. The skin was granular rather than scaly, with rows of limpet-shaped bumps along the belly. The body skin was folded as in large lizards of today. The long, powerful tail was flattened from side to side. A fold of skin, up to 5 inches (12.7 cm) high, formed a mane that extended down the middle of the back and along the top of the tail. Possibly, the mane extended forward up the neck and connected with the crest. The forefeet were webbed, whereas the larger three-toed hind feet had small

hooves with fleshy pads underneath.

*Corythosaurus* and other hadrosaurs had no teeth in the front of their mouths, but small, tightly packed teeth lined the back portion of each jaw. New teeth constantly grew in beneath the old ones, replacing teeth worn out on the chewing surface. The teeth, used to grind up tough plant material, functioned like the efficient, ever-growing teeth of today's cattle, horses, and other grazing animals. One *Corythosaurus* mummy contained fossilized stomach contents including the needles of conifers, twigs, seeds, and fruits of other land plants. Apparently, when it fed, *Corythosaurus* grasped a mouthful of leaves, fruit, or water plants, clamped its flat bill shut, and either tore the materials loose or stripped off the edible portions.

Older reconstructions and mounted skeletons, including the one at Carnegie Museum, show *Corythosaurus* and other hadrosaurs walking with their backs and tails at a 45° angle to the ground. Actually, the structure of the hip sockets and the fact that, in the best preserved hadrosaurs, the back and tail are almost perfectly straight indicate that they walked with their backs nearly horizontal and their tails sticking stiffly out behind. Ossified tendons, a network of thin, bony rods lying along-side the vertebrae of the back and tail, strengthened and stiffened the spine, keeping the heavy body and tail from sagging fore and aft of the hip sockets. The neck curved up, and the head may have bobbed back and forth like a pigeon's when *Corythosaurus* walked.

Studies of *Corythosaurus* and its relatives indicate that *Corythosaurus* did not have a crest throughout its entire life. Quite possibly, the newly hatched and immature *Corythosaurus* had no crest at all; the crest may have developed as the dinosaur reached maturity or may have been more prominent in males.

The purpose of the crest has long intrigued paleontologists. The crest was hollow and housed greatly elongated, convoluted nasal passages. As the dinosaur grew and the nasal passages elongated, the thin and rather fragile bones that enclosed them became distorted and pushed up on top of the head. One theory suggests that enlarged nasal passages gave *Corythosaurus* a very keen sense of smell, perhaps the better with which to detect predators such as *Tyrannosaurus.* The theory also proposes that the complex chamber in the crest may have served the same function as the complicated scrolls of bone in the snouts of mammals. These scrolls, called turbinal bones, are covered with mucous membranes containing nerve endings for the sense of smell. Perhaps in the hollow-crested hadrosaurs this type of smelling apparatus was located on top of the head rather than in the snout.

Other hadrosaur experts dispute this theory. They point out that the nasal capsule (that portion of the nasal passage containing all or most of the scent-sensitive cells) in *Corythosaurus* was not particularly large, resembling in relative size that of modern reptiles; and that the crest was not related to the dinosaur's sense of smell.

Another theory holds that the crests, like antlers of deer, were very helpful in sexual display, that is, in attracting mates. Generally, such display structures do not appear until an animal approaches sexual maturity. This is consistent with conjecture regarding *Corythosaurus*: Their crests possibly did not develop significantly until the individual had achieved a large size. It had been suggested that when *Corythosaurus* wanted to court a female, ward off a rival, or defend a territory, it displayed itself broadside. The frill along the back could have enhanced the illusion of great size. Perhaps the frill and crest were brightly colored to increase the effect.

Recent studies of *Corythosaurus* and related hadrosaurs show that the crests served at least one other function: as a resonating device. The convoluted nasal passages could have made the voice louder and given each of the dinosaurs a distinctive cry. Encounters between rivals or potential mates could be accompanied by loud trumpeting or other cries. If *Corythosaurus* and other hadrosaurs traveled in herds, loud voices would also have helped them to communicate.

Unlike their contemporaries—the horned and armored dinosaurs—hadrosaurs had no armor or horns with which to protect themselves. The structure of the skull, however, does indicate that they had good eyesight and hearing; so *Corythosaurus* can be interpreted as having been constantly on the alert for danger.

Except for *Protoceratops,* remains of newly

hatched dinosaurs were, until recently, rare. Paleontologists often speculated that dinosaurs must have nested in upland areas where remains were unlikely to be fossilized. Recently, however, a dinosaur nesting ground has been found in the Two Medicine Formation of northwestern Montana, deposits the same age as the Oldman Formation in the adjacent province of Alberta, Canada. Although young dinosaurs were found in the Two Medicine Formation as early as 1916 by field parties from the American Museum of Natural History and the Smithsonian Institution, the significance of the deposits was not recognized until 1978. At that time a field crew from Princeton University found the skeletons of eleven baby dinosaurs jumbled together in a bowl-shaped depression on top of a low mound about 9 feet 10 inches (3 m) in diameter and 4 feet 11 inches (1.5 m) wide. Each little skeleton was approximately 39 inches (1 m) long. Portions of four more were scattered nearby. The babies had relatively large hands and feet and short snouts but, otherwise, were proportioned like adult hadrosaurs. Fragments of eggshell were mixed in with the skeletons in the nest cavity. Several hundred feet (100 m) from the nest the crew discovered another group of baby hadrosaurs less than half the size of the others but still associated with large eggshell fragments.

The young hadrosaurs found in the first nest had well-worn teeth and must have grown considerably since they hatched. Also near the nest was found the skull of what may have been a parent. The skull, that of a large hadrosaur with a small pointed cone on its forehead, and the fifteen babies were named *Maiasaura,* which means "good mother reptile." Dinosaurs bearing the greatest resemblance to *Maiasaura* are the crestless duckbills *Anatosaurus* and *Edmontosaurus* that lived at the very end of the Cretaceous.

Field parties returning to Two Medicine in 1979 and 1980 were rewarded with more exciting discoveries. Among the dinosaur remains were more nests, eggs, and hatchlings of hadrosaurs and other dinosaurs.

Eighty percent of dinosaurs collected thus far from the Two Medicine Formation are those of youngsters one-twentieth to one-half the size of adults. If the area were the "dinosaur nursery" it appears to be, hadrosaurs may have cared for their young until they were about half the size of adults.

### Polyglyphanodon

Although dinosaurs were the most conspicuous land animals of the late Cretaceous, many smaller vertebrates also populated the land. Unlike dinosaurs, some of these smaller vertebrates are still alive today. Salamanders and frogs, for example, thrived in the warm climate of the late Cretaceous. Snakes first appeared during the last Cretaceous and, as such, were the latest order of reptiles to evolve. Lizards were not only prevalent during the Cretaceous, but had been around since the late Triassic.

*Polyglyphanodon* is a Cretaceous lizard. It was about 3 feet (0.9 m) long, and its sharp, pointed claws indicate it ran about on land and perhaps climbed trees. A nearly complete skeleton of *Polyglyphanodon* is on exhibit in Dinosaur Hall.

The name *"Polyglyphanodon"* comes from Greek words meaning "many chisel teeth," referring to the sharp, widened teeth at the rear of the jaw that differ from those of any living lizard. The upper and lower teeth interlocked when the jaws were closed. Unlike those in most other reptiles, the teeth were not continuously replaced by new ones. *Polyglyphanodon* was almost certainly a plant-eater.

Between 1937 and 1940, the Smithsonian Institution collected the remains of approximately fifty *Polyglyphanodon* skeletons, some nearly complete, in east-central Utah. All of them were taken out of a single patch of badland not more than a hundred feet (30 m) square. Above and below the layers containing the lizards were found fragmentary dinosaur remains as well as the remains of mammals and two smaller kinds of lizards.

# Dinosaur Latecomers

During the last 6 million years of the Cretaceous, the sea gradually retreated eastward from the north-central United States and south-central Canada, and a vast fresh water lake almost as large as Hudson Bay covered the prairie provinces of Canada. The Rocky Mountains then began to rise again, and the lake was drained and replaced by a series of low hills. Depressions between the hills filled with silt and sand. When the Cretaceous ended, a low, broad floodplain of subtropical forests and numerous small lakes extended east from the Rockies. Here resided *Tyrannosaurus* and *Triceratops,* two of the last dinosaurs to live in what is today Montana and southern Alberta.

### Tyrannosaurus

*Tyrannosaurus* was one of the largest predators known to have walked on land. It was a latecomer to the Age of Reptiles, apparently arriving on the scene towards the end of the Cretaceous, a few million years before all dinosaurs became extinct. In North America *Tyrannosaurus* and its kin, some of which appear earlier in the fossil record, have been found in the states of Montana, Wyoming, South Dakota, and Texas, and in the Canadian province of Alberta. The largest known *Tyrannosaurus, T. bataar,* was found in Mongolia, and other medium-sized tyrannosaurs have been discovered in India, China, and Mongolia. Skeletal fragments have also been found in Argentina.

Carnegie Museum's mounted *Tyrannosaurus* skeleton stands 18 feet (5.5 m) high and is 47 feet (14.1 m) long from the tip of the snout to the end of the tail. In life, it is estimated to have weighed about 7½ tons (7500 kg). The skull of the skeleton alone measures an impressive 4 feet (1.2 m). Its many large openings reduce its overall weight. Along the margins of the jaws of *Tyrannosaurus* are dagger-shaped teeth, each of which is up to 6 inches (15 cm) long. Tiny serrations along the front and back of each tooth increased its effectiveness in slicing through flesh. Only a very small portion of the upper rear part of *Tyrannosaurus'* skull was occupied by its brain.

*Above: Skull of* Tyrannosaurus rex *(C.M. Vertebrate Fossil No. 9380). Dagger-shaped teeth, up to 6 inches long, dotted the margins of the powerful jaw of* Tyrannosaurus. *Tiny serrations along the front and back of each tooth increased its effectiveness for cutting through flesh.* **Left:** *Forelimbs of* Tyrannosaurus rex *(C.M. Vertebrate Fossil No. 9380). These tiny forelimbs are dwarfed by the rest of the massive and powerful body. They may have served to grasp and manipulate prey and morsels of flesh. The* Tyrannosaurus *painting is a portion of a mural done by Ottmar F. von Fuehrer.*

Its great body weight was supported by massive hind legs and hip bones. The proportions of the hind legs, along with the enormous size and weight of the body, indicate that *Tyrannosaurus* was not an agile or fast runner; it probably walked slowly, rocking from side to side with each step.

In contrast to the massive hind legs, the front legs of *Tyrannosaurus* were tiny and surely not used for walking. Although lower arm bones and hands of *Tyrannosaurus* have never been found, other related dinosaurs are known to have had only two functional fingers, each armed with a claw. The tiny forelegs were probably used to grasp and manipulate prey and pieces of flesh. Healed fractures indicate that *Tyrannosaurus* frequently injured its upper arm bone; perhaps they were crushed by the weight of their massive bodies.

The tail of *Tyrannosaurus* was long and powerful. Since no complete tail has been found, no one knows positively just how long the tail grew. When walking, *Tyrannosaurus* did not drag its tail on the ground. Its body may have been held more or less horizontally with the tail held stiffly, straight out behind the body.

Many reptiles have abdominal ribs, and those of *Tyrannosaurus* are especially prominent. In the skeleton in Dinosaur Hall, two pairs of ribs have been mounted on the upper chest, between the front legs. In life, *Tyrannosaurus* had other ribs below these.

As its name, Greek words for "tyrant lizard," suggests, *Tyrannosaurus* was a formidable predator. It would probably grasp the neck of an unarmored duck-billed dinosaur, an easy prey, and blood vessels and nerves or even the spinal column were broken. While devouring its victim, *Tyrannosaurus* may have held the carcass down with its hind feet while it ripped off pieces with its jaws.

In addition to the duck-billed dinosaurs, other plant-eating dinosaurs probably were preyed upon by *Tyrannosaurus*. Herbivores probably relied on their body armor—club, plates, and spikes—as well as on the ability to flee to defend themselves. *Tyrannosaurus* also sometimes got into fights with others of its own kind. One *Tyrannosaurus,* for example, was found with injured vertebrae; another had broken ribs and a punctured jaw. The jaw wound, partially healed before the victim died, appears to have been inflicted by another *Tyrannosaurus*.

Little is known about reproduction of *Tyrannosaurus*. It may have laid eggs or borne its young alive. One dinosaur expert studied the proportional changes in the bone length of six half-grown to fully grown skeletons of a relative of *Tyrannosaurus* found in Canada, *Albertosaurus*. According to the calculations, a baby *Albertosaurus* stood about 26 inches (66 cm) high and was approximately 36 inches (91 cm) long. It had very long hind legs, a slender body, and a small head compared to that of adults. It could not overcome an adult horned dinosaur or duck-bill, of course, but the baby *Albertosaurus* must have been very fast and agile enough to pursue small, active prey such as lizards, snakes, frogs, and other small dinosaurs. Perhaps it sometimes dined on birds or the small, primitive mammals that shared its habitat.

All members of the family to which *Tyrannosaurus* belonged are known definitely only from the late Cretaceous; all had similar skeletons. Superficially, they all resembled larger versions of *Allosaurus,* but major differences lead many dinosaur experts to believe that they cannot be direct descendents.

The remains of tyrannosaurs are not commonly found. They were probably outnumbered, as large predators are today, by the animals they preyed upon. The *Tyrannosaurus* skeleton in Dinosaur Hall is one of only five such skeletons ever found. It was collected in 1902 and 1903 by a field party from the American Museum of Natural History. When it was excavated in Hell Creek in eastern Montana, most of the neck vertebrae and forelimbs and all of the tail were missing. In 1941, George H. Clapp, a Carnegie Institute trustee, purchased the *Tyrannosaurus* skeleton for the Museum. It was mounted and put on display in 1942.

*Below:* Skull of Triceratops brevicornus *(C.M. Vertebrate Fossil No. 1219), a horned dinosaur of the Cretaceous. Three horns grew from the snout and above each eye. In life, the bony neck frill may have been fringed with spines. Such armament helped ward off* Tyrannosaurus *and other predators.* **Left:** W.H. Utterback collected this Triceratops *skull in the Lance Formation near Hell Creek, Montana. He is shown here preparing the specimen.*

## Triceratops

The large horned dinosaurs, belonging to the family Ceratopsidae, within the suborder of ceratopsians, were partially equipped with armor to ward off *Tyrannosaurus* and other predators. These ceratopsians had bony necks frills that were sometimes fringed with spines. They also had one to three horns growing from the snout and above each of the eyes. *Triceratops* and *Torosaurus,* the largest of the family of ceratopsids, were two of the last known dinosaurs to inhabit the earth.

Hundreds of *Triceratops* skulls have been found throughout western North America—in the states of Montana, Wyoming, Colorado, and South Dakota and in the Canadian provinces of Alberta and Saskatchewan. The *Triceratops* skull exhibited in Dinosaur Hall was found in eastern Montana in 1904 and was collected by Carnegie Museum paleontologist W.H. Utterback.

Carnegie Museum's *Triceratops* skull is about 6 feet and 3 inches (1.9 m) long, an average size for members of this genus. The largest skull known, 8 feet (2.4 m) long, is mounted on a skeleton exhibited in the American Museum of Natural History. Some adult *Triceratops* reached a length of more than 25 feet (7.65 m), with the skull accounting for one third of the total body length, and measured 9½ feet (3 m) from the ground to the hips.

On the *Triceratops* skull, there are two stout brow horns above the eyes, and another shorter horn is on the tip of the snout. In life, these horns were covered with horny sheaths that made them even longer. A thick, upturned frill grew from the back of the skull and covered the neck.

*Triceratops* had a huge, parrot-like beak. It had no teeth in the front of its mouth, but the rear portion of each jaw was lined with densely packed, small teeth, between thirty-six and forty in each upper and lower tooth row. For all practical purposes, the teeth were so close that they seemed to form a long, unbroken chewing surface. A single rib in the middle of each tooth gave the cutting edge of the toothrows a jagged outline. As in all ceratopsians, the teeth sheared past each other on a vertical plane, functioning somewhat like a double pair of pinking shears, and must have been capable of chopping up very tough plant fibers. To keep the food from falling

out of their mouths while they chewed, ceratopsians probably had cheeks.

Teeth were continuously replaced in ceratopsians. Three or four replacement teeth grew in the jaws above or below each small tooth. When an old tooth wore down, it fell out, revealing a new, unworn tooth beneath it. *Triceratops,* thus, enjoyed good teeth throughout its life. Altogether, as many as 640 teeth may have lined its mouth at one time. Unfortunately, the teeth are missing from Carnegie Museum's *Triceratops* skull, but the vertical troughs where the tooth columns once grew can be seen.

*Triceratops* and other ceratopsians had a tooth arrangement generally similar to that of *Corythosaurus.* The arrangements differed, however, in that the teeth met at different angles. The ceratopsians could only cut and chop their food, while the hadrosaurs, with upper and lower tooth rows meeting on an inclined plane, did more crushing. What *Triceratops* and its kin ate is uncertain. The arrangement of their teeth would seem to indicate they could chew tough, fibrous leaves of cycads and palms as well as other plants and fruits.

The body of *Triceratops* was massive with a rather short tail for a dinosaur. The rhinoceros-like feet had toes ending in small hooves. *Triceratops* and other large ceratopsians probably were poor swimmers. It is hard to imagine how they could have kept their heavy heads above water. *Triceratops* probably spent most of its life in savannah-like country.

*Triceratops* possibly defended itself in part by traveling about in herds. Even a giant *Tyrannosaurus* would hesitate to attack a group of these horned beasts especially since, in spite of its heavy, lumbering body, it may have been capable of short bursts of speed. A charging *Triceratops* would be nothing to be trifled with!

The family of ceratopsids to which *Triceratops* belongs is believed to have evolved from a dinosaur like *Protoceratops* that came into western North America from Asia. Except for a couple of dubious bone fragments from Mongolia, ceratopsids are known only in western North America. Their evolutionary history was relatively short, lasting approximately 10 to 11 million years.

All were quadrupeds, but many variations in horn development and frill shape were evident. In many of the more advanced ceratopsians, the frill became larger, and, as with *Protoceratops,* openings in the bony frill were sometimes present. In contrast, *Triceratops* had a relatively short frill composed of solid bone.

Some ceratopsids had a long, stout nose horn; others had two long brow horns and a very short nose horn. Still others had three well-developed horns. *Styracosaurus* had several extra horns growing from the rim of its frill. *Pachyrhinosaurus* apparently had no horns, but a thick, bony swelling grew on its snout and extended back to its eyes.

Within the more than eleven described species of *Triceratops,* their size and the length of the horns varies considerably. Some *Triceratops* had long brow horns; others, short. In some the nose horn was very short, but in others it was well developed. Possibly, some of these variations are due to differences in age or sex.

Those who have studied ceratopsids have speculated on what value the frills and horns may have held in life. The earliest theory proposed that they were for defense against predators. Later, students tried to demonstrate that the muscles that closed the jaws were attached to the frill and discounted the frill's defensive function. They argued that the increase in the size of the frill primarily permitted the attachment of larger muscles that consequently increased the strength of the bite. A subsequent study of the mechanics and leverage of available ceratopsian jaws, however, failed to demonstrate any mechanical advantage in a lengthened frill.

Neither theory adequately explains why a variety of frill and horn types evolved while the rest of the ceratopsian body remained basically the same. More recent studies have led to a new theory suggesting that the various frill and horn arrays were social adaptations used in courtship and contests for territory. In a dominance contest, rivals may have pushed with their heads. The solid frill would usually have protected the fighters from serious injury. Eventually, the weaker of the two would be likely to give up and retreat, leaving the victor in charge of the contested territory and/or the females.

Paleontologists know for certain that ceratopsids did put their horns and frills to use. In some fossils, the horns had been broken during the lifetime of the animal. Occasionally, a horned dinosaur's skull and frill are scarred with old, healed wounds. The wounds of the skull of one *Torosaurus,* for example, apparently turned into lesions.

*Triceratops* and other large ceratopsids stood with their elbows bent out and their front legs spread wide apart, giving them a wide base of support for pushing and shoving. When *Triceratops* lowered its head so that its brow horns pointed straight ahead, the lines of force went straight through the horns and through the occipital condyle (the joint between the head and neck). In *Triceratops* there were chambers beneath the brow horns formed by overgrowths of the paired bones that normally form a single layer over the eyes. These chambers may have been analogous to the large sinuses or cavities found inside the skulls under the horns of big horn sheep and goats of today. In the sheep and goats, these sinuses cushion blows from head-on crashes. Perhaps the chambers in *Triceratops* functioned in a similar way.

# Reptile Relatives: Birds and Mammals

The Mesozoic is well characterized as the Age of Reptiles, for, throughout these millions of years, reptiles filled the land, water and sky. Not only did the dinosaurs dominate the land, but the reptilian mosasaurs, plesiosaurs, and ichthyosaurs were prominent sea dwellers and the winged pterosaurs were important in the air. In addition to these, still other reptiles flourished during the Mesozoic. Among them were the ancestors of the birds and the mammals.

Birds are closely related to dinosaurs. Their evolutionary relationship has prompted one authority to comment, not entirely in jest, that all dinosaurs are not extinct but that some live on as birds! For a long time it has been recognized that birds resembled the thecodonts, the reptilian ancestors of the dinosaurs. Recent reinterpretation of *Archaeopteryx,* the oldest known bird of the late Jurassic, strengthens the theory that birds are descended not just from the thecodonts but actually from some small, active theropod dinosaurs. Although experts continue to debate the exact affinities of dinosaurs and birds, under any theory, the birds must be reckoned as among the closest, though highly modified, relatives of the dinosaurs.

In contrast, mammal origins are not so clearly traced. By the late Paleozoic, the reptilian subclass Synapsida had already diverged from other reptilian groups. Among Mesozoic synapsids, several lines became more mammalian in structure with the first mammals appearing in the late Triassic.

Throughout the Mesozoic, these mammals were mostly small. Some were herbivorous, filling a somewhat rodent-like role; others were insectivorous and omnivorous. By the end of the Cretaceous, the mammals had undergone some diversification, with several types in existence. They did not, however, reach their height of diversity and dominance until after the great reptile extinction at the end of the Cretaceous.

***Page 108:*** Archaeopteryx, *the earliest known bird. This late Jurassic bird is believed to have descended from small theropod dinosaurs. Archaeopteryx was about the size of a pigeon and had clawed forefeet and hind feet. Skeletal characteristics suggest that it was a poor flier. This original watercolor by Rudolf Freund first appeared in an article by Dr. Kenneth C. Parkes in* Living Bird.

# Why Did the Dinosaurs Become Extinct?

## Casualties and Survivors

At the close of the Cretaceous, a great wave of extinctions swept the earth, affecting life both on the land and in the sea. It has been estimated that as many as seventy-five percent of the species of plants and animals living at the end of the Cretaceous failed to survive into the succeeding Cenozoic. The dinosaurs were the most obvious casualties, but other large reptiles—the mosasaurs, the plesiosaurs, the giant sea turtles, and the last of the ichthyosaurs—disappeared from the sea, and pterosaurs disappeared from the sky. The Age of Reptiles was over.

Although the large vertebrates were gone, many smaller land vertebrates survived the crisis. Mammals, birds, amphibians and reptiles such as crocodilians, lizards, turtles, and snakes lived on to form the nucleus of vertebrate life on earth as we know it today.

## Theories

A number of theories have been developed to explain the sudden extinction. Some believe that gradual environmental changes were the ultimate cause. Others believe that the mass extinctions were caused by a sudden global catastrophe.

Those who attribute the extinctions to gradual environmental changes contend that, during the latter part of the late Cretaceous, average temperatures steadily declined. During this period, the "gradualists" point out, many species of primitive plants (cycads, tree-ferns, araucarians) that require warmer temperatures were replaced in higher latitudes by hardier trees (redwoods, cedars, bald cypress). These changes in vegetation suggest, according to the gradualists, a global cooling to which dinosaurs, unlike warm-blooded bird and mammals, could not adapt. As suitable habitat slowly disappeared, so did the dinosaurs.

The cooler temperatures may have been a by-product of continental drift. As continents continued to drift apart, the land and sea relationships were altered. The warm, shallow seas that once covered much of the interior of the continent began to withdraw, perhaps forcing large marine reptiles into hostile, cooler seas in which they could not survive.

Gradualists claim that the fossil record of the dinosaurs indicates that they were on the decline for several million years before they finally became extinct. Other theorists state that the reason fewer dinosaurs are known from the end of the Cretaceous is not because they were more scarce, but because fewer paleontologists have searched for them.

In contrast to the gradualists, others known as "catastrophists" emphasize the *sudden* disappearance from the fossil record, not only of the larger vertebrates, but of many forms of floating marine plankton as well. These theorists contend that the global extinctions at the end of the Cretaceous were every bit as dramatic and sudden as, indeed, they seem to have been.

One intriguing catastrophic theory, the "Alverez-asteroid Model," draws upon some indirect geological evidence. The theory states that a large asteroid or meteorite, perhaps ten miles in diameter, struck the earth. On impact, it disintegrated and, in doing so, created a cloud of dust debris so dense that it cut off light from the sun until it dissipated some two or three years later.

During this time, plant life, dependent upon sunlight, died. This led to the death of all herbivorous terrestrial and marine animals and their predators. Whole ecosystems collapsed. Vegetation eventually re-established itself from dormant seeds, spores and sprouts, but the large, plant-eating dinosaurs and their meat-eating cousins were gone forever.

The "Alverez-asteroid Model" is based upon the finding that a thin layer of clay located precisely at the Cretaceous/Cenozoic boundary in sedimentary rock is abnormally high in the heavy metal iridium. The composition of this layer appears to be a worldwide phenomenon. Iridium is extremely rare in sedimentary rocks and only by postulating an extra-terrestrial origin, say the Alverez team, can one account for this dramatic increase in iridium content of the boundary clay.

No crater that could be attributed to such a collision has ever been found. According to the Alverez team, however, the incoming asteroid may have landed in the ocean or exploded in the air. It has even been theorized that a direct hit on a mid-oceanic rift would produce a great, prolonged up-welling of lava. The volcanic activity present around Iceland may represent an example of what could be initiated by such an action.

Other theorists attribute the mass extinction to the explosion of a supernova that would kill by radiation. Still others claim that a global catastrophe was brought on by a sudden release of cold, polar sea water into warm southern oceans. Possible changes in the conformation of the Arctic Ocean basin may have produced the polar water spill-over and consequent changes in global climatic patterns.

Despite the wealth of theories, there are few real facts. Those who advocate slow environmental changes must yet explain the sheer magnitude of the Great Extinction in what seems to have been a relatively short period of time. Those who champion catastrophes must find some direct evidence on a trail of history already 70 million years cold.

# About Geologic Time, The History of Life on Earth and Scientific Names

## Geologic Time

Museum visitors are often curious about the age of a fossil—whether it be a dinosaur or some other form of prehistoric life. They are surprised when the age is given, not in the number of years ago the organism lived, but in geologic time terms such as "early Jurassic" or "late Triassic."

Such time terms, first established by geologists of the late eighteenth and the nineteenth centuries, were developed primarily through studies of sedimentary rocks and the fossils they contain. It was noted that, when undisturbed, a sequence of layered, sedimentary rock represented successively younger rock layers. The fossils found within each successive layer were younger than those found in earlier layers. Thus, in undisturbed sedimentary rock layers, the oldest fossils would be found in the lowest layers, whereas the youngest would be found in the upper-most layers.

Gradually, the now-accepted subdivisions of geologic time developed. Geologic time began with a long Precambrian interval and was followed by the Paleozoic, Mesozoic and Cenozoic Eras.

Early in the twentieth century, when it was discovered that rocks contain radioactive elements that progressively decayed over time, ages in years began to be applied with scientific accuracy to the geologic time scale. Through a technique called radiometric dating, the radioactive decay that had occurred in certain elements in a rock could be measured and used to determine the rock's age. The age could then be incorporated into the geologic time scale, providing an overall framework for the study of life on earth.

## The History of Life on Earth: A Quick Summary

The history of the earth encompasses an immense period of time—almost inconceivable from our own approximately seventy-year life span. The earth is now estimated to be about 4.6 billion years old. The first known life, simple one-celled organisms, dates back to about 3.5 billion years. Around 570 million years ago, in the Cambrian Period, at the beginning of the Paleozoic Era, a multitude of invertebrate animals, mostly hard-shelled, appeared in the fossil record. The first vertebrates made their appearance during the following period, the Ordovician. By the end of the Silurian, a very important event occurred: Plants moved onto land. The next interval, the Devonian Period, is noted for its diversity of fish and for concluding with the move of amphibians onto land. The following period, the Mississippian, is highlighted by the appearance of reptiles.

The Mesozoic Era, known as the Age of Reptiles, is the focal point for this book. During the span of this era, from 247 to 65 million years ago,[14] the dinosaurs originated, flourished, and finally became extinct.

The Cenozoic Era, which began about 65 million years ago and is still technically the era in which we live, is a dinosaur-less time. Known as the Age of Mammals, the Cenozoic witnessed the appearance of modern man approximately 30,000 years ago—a moment from yesterday in geologic time!

Reading this book from the perspective of the earth's history, you will begin to realize how lucky we are to have discovered the dinosaurs bones at all. Mere newcomers to the earth millions of years after the last dinosaur vanished, humankind could have lost to erosion the chance to uncover one of earth's most monumental secrets—its Age of Reptiles.

## Scientific Names

Biologists classify all known living things, including those that are now extinct, in a hierarchical scheme designed to reflect what is known about how they evolved and their relationship to other forms of life. Structure, behavior, genetics, and fossil history are considered in deciding the category. Because there is still much to learn, classifications are often revised.

Each life form is classified in at least seven categories, each more restrictive than the preceding one: the kingdom, the phylum, the class, the order, the family, the genus, and the species. For an example of how the system works, examine how *Diplodocus* would be classified: Kingdom: Animalia (animal); Phylum: Chordata (animals with a backbone); Class: Reptilia (reptile); Order: Saurischia (reptile-hipped dinosaur); Family: Diplodocidae; Genus: *Diplodocus;* Species: *carnegii.*

The combination of the generic (genus) and specific (species) names is the scientific name by which a particular organism is known. Most of the names are derived from Latin or Greek words that describe the plant or animal, refer to the locality where it was collected, or perpetuate the name of a person the describer wished to commemorate. The genus name *"Diplodocus,"* for example, is Latin for "double-beamed," and the species name *"carnegii"* was given in honor of Andrew Carnegie. Modern man is *"Homo sapiens,"* "man of thought"; and the alligator is *"Alligator mississippiensis,"* "Mississippi alligator."

Scientists usually use the complete scientific name (genus and species) when referring to a plant or animal. Unfortunately, vertebrate paleontologists, especially dinosaur students, usually have only fragmentary skeletons to work with and find it difficult to distinguish one species from another. For this reason, generally, only generic names are used in this book.

The following outline classification of the dinosaurs mentioned in the book is no exception. Generic names of the dinosaurs are categorized within their increasingly restricted order. For the sake of simplicity only the two references in the text to specific families, (Protoceratopidae and Ceratopidae) are listed.

**Order Saurischia**

    Suborder Theropoda
        Infraorder Coelurosauria
            *Compsognathus*
            *Coelophysis*
        Infraorder Carnosauria
            *Megalosaurus*
            *Allosaurus*
            *Ceratosaurus*
            *Albertosaurus*
            *Tyrannosaurus*

    Suborder Sauropodomorpha
        Infraorder Prosauropoda
            *Plateosaurus*
        Infraorder Sauropoda
            *Cetiosaurus*
            *Diplodocus*
            *Apatosaurus*
            *Camarasaurus*
            *Hypselosaurus*
            *Barosaurus*
            *Brachiosaurus*

**Order Ornithischia**

    Suborder Ornithopoda
        *Dryosaurus*
        *Hypsilophodon*
        *Camptosaurus*
        *Iguanodon*
        *Trachodon*
        *Corythosaurus*
        *Hadrosaurus*

    Suborder Ceratopsia
        *Protoceratops* (Protoceratopidae)
        *Triceratops* (Ceratopidae)

    Suborder Stegosauria
        *Stegosaurus*

    Suborder Ankylosauria
        *Ankylosaurus*

**Key**

**Triassic**
  1. marine and fresh-water Triassic fossils
  2. *Metoposaurus* skulls
**Jurassic**
  3. marine Jurassic fossils
• 4. *Allosaurus*
• 5. *Stegosaurus*
• 6. *Diplodocus*
  7. *Diplodocus* thigh bone
• 8. *Apatosaurus*
• 9. *Camptosaurus*
• 10. *Dryosaurus*
  11. *Camarasaurus* skull
  12. *Diplodocus* skull
  13. *Diplodocus* skull and neck vertebrae
• 14. young *Camarasaurus*
  15. Jurassic pterosaurs
**Cretaceous**
  16. Marine Cretaceous fossils
  17. *Polyglyphanodon*
  18. Cretaceous foliage
• 19. *Protoceratops*
  20. *Tyrannosaurus rex* skull
  21. *Tyrannosaurus rex* teeth
  22. *Triceratops* skull
• 23. *Tyrannosaurus rex*
  24. mural of *Tyrannosaurus rex*
• 25. *Corythosaurus*
  26. Cretaceous pterosaurs
  27. mural of Kansas' Niobrara Sea

• = *Carnegie's complete dinosaur skeletons*

# Floorplan

Cenozoic Hall

**Dinosaur Hall**

Paleozoic Hall

# Glossary

**Age of Reptiles:** An informal name given to the time (the Mesozoic Era) during which dinosaurs and other reptiles were the dominant life forms.

**Ammonite:** A group (Subclass Ammonoidea) of tentacled molluscs (Phylum Mollusca, Class Cephalopoda) with a coiled and chambered shell. Their fossil record begins in the Devonian, and they were very abundant in Mesozoic seas, but became extinct at the close of the Cretaceous.

**Amphibian:** One of the classes (Amphibia) of vertebrate animals. Unlike reptiles, amphibians must lay their eggs in water. Living amphibians include frogs, toads, salamanders and caecilians. The oldest fossil amphibians have been recovered from late Devonian rocks in Greenland.

**Ankylosaur:** A group (Suborder Ankylosauria) of ornithischian (bird-hipped) dinosaurs commonly known as the armored dinosaurs because much of their body was covered by an armor composed of bony plates. Ankylosaurs lived throughout the Cretaceous Period and were herbivorous and quadrupedal.

**Arthropod:** A group of animals, including the living horseshoe crabs, scorpions, spiders, ticks, mites, insects, centipedes, millipedes and crustaceans (crabs, lobsters, shrimp, crayfish) as well as the fossil trilobites, that compose the Phylum Arthropoda. Arthropods, with over 800,000 described species, comprise about eighty percent of all known animal species, and, among invertebrates (animals without a backbone) have developed the most successful adaptations to life on land and in the air. The fossil record of arthropods extends back to the Paleozoic Era.

**Asteroid:** A small, interplanetary body of rock which was formed at the same time and by the same process as planets. Asteroids are essentially tiny planets with elliptical orbits in the solar system. The asteroid belt occurs between Mars and Jupiter. Some asteroids (called Apollo asteroids) have orbits that cross the orbit of the earth.

**Bipedal:** Standing, walking or running on the two hind limbs. Bipedal dinosaurs include the theropods and ornithopods.

**Bivalve:** (Clam) A group of molluscs. The bodies of these animals are enclosed in two shells that are hinged together. Another name for bivalves is pelecypods.

**Brachiopod:** A group of invertebrate animals (Phylum Brachiopoda) commonly known as lamp shells. They superficially resemble bivalves in having a two-valved shell, but are actually not closely related to them. Brachiopods are fixed to the sea bottom by a stalk or by one of the shells. They were among the dominant members of sea-bottom faunas during the Paleozoic, but have declined in number and diversity since

then, and only a few species survive today.

**Carnivore:** A meat-eater. Among dinosaurs, typical carnivores were *Allosaurus* and *Tyrannosaurus*.

**Catastrophist:** A person or theory holding that physical or organic change during the history of the earth is due to sudden, violent changes on the earth's surface.

**Cenozoic Era:** The last of the eras (following Paleozoic and Mesozoic) into which the history of life on earth is divided. Cenozoic means "era of modern life" and is often referred to as the "Age of Mammals." It lasted from approximately 65 million years ago to the present.

**Cephalopod:** A class of animals in the Phylum Mollusca including octopi, squids and cuttle fish, as well as shelled forms, such as the extinct ammonites and coleoids.

**Ceratopsian:** A group (Suborder Ceratopsia) of ornithischian (bird-hipped) dinosaurs commonly referred to as the horned dinosaurs. Ceratopsians lived during the late Cretaceous and were herbivorous and quadrupedal. As the name "horned dinosaurs" implies, some ceratopsians bore horns over the eye and nose regions of the skull, and a frill, or shield, of bone extended from the back of the skull over the neck. Like all other dinosaurs, ceratopsians became extinct at the end of the Cretaceous.

**Clutch:** A nest of eggs.

**Coleoids:** A group (Subclass Coleoidea) of molluscs in the Class Cephalopoda. Coleoids either lack shells or have internal ones. They are known from the Mississippian Period to the present. Living ones are octopi and squids.

**Cretaceous Period:** The youngest period of the Mesozoic Era (after the Triassic and Jurassic), from approximately 143 to 65 million years ago. Many organisms, including dinosaurs, became extinct at the end of the Cretaceous.

**Crocodilian:** One of the groups of reptiles (Order Crocodilia) in the subclass Archosauria. Crocodilians first appeared in the mid-Triassic and became diverse and abundant in the Mesozoic and Cenozoic. Unlike other archosaurian reptiles (dinosaurs, pterosaurs), crocodilians survived the wave of extinctions at the end of the Cretaceous.

**Crustaceans:** A class of animals in the Phylum Arthropoda including the living crabs, shrimp, lobsters, crayfish, wood lice, barnacles and water fleas. They are known from the Cambrian Period to the Recent.

**Diapsid:** A condition in some reptiles in which two openings (called temporal openings) occur on either side of the skull. This condition is present in archosaurs and lepidosaurs, two groups often referred to as diapsid reptiles.

**Dinosaur:** A name meaning "terrible lizard" that describes a group of gigantic reptiles that dominated life on land during the Mesozoic Era. The term "dinosaur" includes two distinct groups: the Saurischia (reptile-hipped dinosaurs) and the Ornithischia (bird-hipped dinosaurs). Both groups of dinosaurs became extinct at the end of the Cretaceous Period.

**Djadochta Formation:** The name given to a specific body of rock (or geologic formation) that was deposited in Mongolia during the late Cretaceous. These rocks preserve skeletal remains of many late Cretaceous dinosaurs and mammals. Possibly the most famous fossil occurrences in the Djadochta Formation are the skeletons of the ceratopsian dinosaur *Protoceratops* found in association with fossilized nests of eggs.

**Echinoderms:** A group of invertebrate animals (Phylum Echinodermata) that are exclusively marine and include the living sea stars, sea cucumbers, sea urchins, sea lilies, starfish, basket stars, brittle stars and sand dollars. They are known in the fossil record since the Cambrian Period.

**Ectotherm:** An organism, often called "cold-blooded," that relies on the external environment (such as the sun's rays) to control its internal temperature. Among vertebrates, fish, amphibians and reptiles are ectotherms.

**Endotherm:** An organism, often called "warm-blooded," that garners its heat from internal metabolic sources, rather than from the external environment. The internal temperature of an endotherm is controlled physiologically despite variations in external tempertures. Among vertebrates, mammals and birds are endotherms.

**Fossil:** Any remains of an organism, or evidence of its presence, preserved in rocks. Usually hard parts of organisms are preserved but other kinds of fossil occurrences include impressions, casts and footprints.

**Gradualist:** A person or theory holding that physical or organic change during the history of the earth is due to slow, gradual changes on the earth's surface.

**Hadrosaur:** A group of ornithischian (bird-hipped) dinosaurs that appeared in the late Cretaceous and are commonly known as the duck-billed dinosaurs. They had webbed feet and a duck-like muzzle and were probably semi-aquatic and herbivorous. Some hadrosaurs had bony crests on their heads that were either solid or hollow with air passages.

**Herbivore:** A plant-eater. Herbivorous dinosaurs include the

sauropods and most ornithischians.

**Holzmaden:** A quarry in southern Germany in early Jurassic black shales that has yielded very well preserved remains of invertebrates, plesiosaurs, ichthyosaurs and fishes.

**Hypsilophodontid:** A family of ornithischian (bird-hipped) dinosaurs that are known in the fossil record from the late Triassic to the early Cretaceous. They were small- to medium-sized herbivorous dinosaurs and either bipedal or quadrupedal.

**Ichthyosaur:** A group of marine reptiles that were diverse in the Mesozoic but became extinct in the Cretaceous. Ichthyosaurs inhabited the open seas, had a streamlined, dolphin-like body, long jaws with numerous teeth, and limbs modified into paddles. They gave birth to live young, so that, unlike other reptiles, they did not have to leave the water to reproduce.

**Invertebrate:** All animals that lack a vertebral column (a backbone). These include the protozoans (one-celled animals), sponges, corals and jellyfish, flatworms, roundworms, segmented worms, molluscs, arthropods, brachiopods, echinoderms, hemichordates, tunicates and arrowworms.

**Jurassic Period:** The middle period (between the Triassic and Cretaceous) of the Mesozoic Era, from approximately 212 to 143 million years ago.

**Lizard:** A group of diapsid reptiles closely related to snakes. They first appear in the fossil record in the late Triassic. Lizards, snakes, *Sphenodon* and a variety of extinct groups compose the Subclass Lepidosauria, one of the major groups of reptiles.

**Mammal:** One of the classes (Class Mammalia) of vertebrate animals including the living monotremes, marsupials and placentals. Some distinguishing features of mammals are endothermy, hair, mammary glands, a diaphragm, four-chambered heart, upright stance, differentiated teeth, and differentiated vertebrae. Mammals evolved from synapsid reptiles in the late Triassic and became the dominant terrestrial vertebrates in the Cenozoic, after the extinction of the dinosaurs.

**Mesozoic Era:** The middle era of earth's life history (between the older Paleozoic and the younger Cenozoic) extending from approximately 247 to 65 million years ago, and commonly called the "Age of Reptiles". It is divided into three periods: Triassic, Jurassic and Cretaceous, from oldest to youngest.

**Meteorite:** Small body of matter from interplanetary space that has entered the earth's atmosphere and fallen to the surface of the earth. Strictly speaking, a meteorite is that portion of a meteor that manages to reach the earth's surface.

**Molluscs:** A group of invertebrate animals (Phylum Mollusca) which includes the bivalves (clams), gastropods (snails), squids and octopi and their fossil relatives.

**Morrison Formation:** The name given to a specific body of rock that was deposited during the late Jurassic and early Cretaceous over a widespread area of the western United States. These rocks are famous for the excellent preservation of many late Jurassic and early Cretaceous dinosaurs, and especially the sauropods, including *Diplodocus* and *Apatosaurus*. Dinosaur National Monument in Utah is set in the Morrison Formation.

**Mosasaur:** A group of aquatic fossil lizards that lived in late Cretaceous seas and achieved gigantic size.

**Nothosaur:** An extinct group of semi-aquatic and fully aquatic reptiles that inhabited Triassic seas and resembled plesiosaurs in skeletal structure, except for the lack of paddle-like limbs.

**Oldman Formation:** A geologic formation (or body of rock) that was deposited during the late Cretaceous in the southern portion of Alberta. Rocks of the Oldman Formation are famous for preserving a variety of late Cretaceous dinosaurs and mammals. Many of the badlands of the Oldman Formation make up Dinosaur Provincial Park in Alberta.

**Ornithischian:** The group (Order Ornithischia) of bird-hipped dinosaurs, including ornithopods, ceratopsians, ankylosaurs and stegosaurs. Ornithischian dinosaurs are characterized by having a bird-like, four-pronged pelvis.

**Ornithopod:** A group (Suborder Ornithopoda) of ornithischian (bird-hipped) dinosaurs that is known in the fossil record from the middle Triassic to the late Cretaceous. There are seven distinct families of ornithopods, of which the most familiar are the hadrosaurs (duck-billed dinosaurs), and pachycephalosaurs (dome-headed dinosaurs). All ornithopods were herbivorous and bipedal.

**Oxbow:** A crescent-shaped lake formed in a river bend, which, by a change in the course of the river, has become separated from the main river channel.

**Paleontologist:** A scientist who studies the life of past geological ages through the study of fossil remains of organisms.

**Paleozoic Era:** The first era in the history of life on earth. It means "period of ancient life" and extends from about 570 to 247 million years ago. It has been divided into a number of geologic periods, which, from oldest to youngest are: Cambrian, Ordovician, Silurian, Devonian, Carboniferous and Permian.

**Pangaea:** The name of the supercontinent that started to split apart in the Triassic.

**Pelecypods:** See Bivalve.

**Plesiosaur:** An extinct group of aquatic reptiles that flourished during the Mesozoic. They had barrel-shaped bodies, limbs modified into paddles, and either short necks and long heads or long necks and short heads. Plesiosaurs, some of which achieved a size of 50 feet, swam in open seas by means of their paddle-like limbs.

**Prosauropod:** One of the two groups (Infraorder Prosauropoda) of sauropodomorph saurischian (reptile-hipped) dinosaurs. They are known in the fossil record from the mid-Triassic to the early Jurassic. Prosauropods are thought to have been ancestral to the sauropods.

**Pterodactyl:** One group of the "winged-reptiles," the Pterosauria. Pterodactyls lived during the Jurassic and Cretaceous Periods and ranged in size from that of a sparrow *(Pterodactylus)* to forms with a 40-foot wingspan. They relied mostly on soaring flight and somewhat on powered flight. Pterodactyls became extinct before the end of the Cretaceous.

**Pterosaur:** A group (Order Pterosauria) of archosaurian reptiles that evolved gliding, soaring and flying abilities. Their wing was a membrane stretched between the ankles and a greatly elongated fourth finger of the hand. There is evidence that some pterosaurs were covered with a fur-like, scale-like or feather-like skin. Two main groups of pterosaurs evolved: the more primitive rhamphorhynchoids, which were exclusively Jurassic and retained the long, reptilian tail; and the more advanced pterodactyls, which lived during the Jurassic and Cretaceous and developed longer wings and a much reduced tail.

**Quadrupedal:** Standing, walking or running on all four limbs. Sauropods, stegosaurs, ankylosaurs and ceratopsians were quadrupedal dinosaurs.

**Quarry:** A surface excavation from which rocks, building stones, or fossils are extracted.

**Reptile:** One of the classes (Class Reptilia) of vertebrate animals. Living reptiles include crocodiles (Order Crocodilia), lizards and snakes (Order Squamata), *Sphenodon* (Order Rhynchocephalia), and turtles (Order Chelonia). All reptiles, both fossil and living, are divided into six subclasses: Anapsida (primitive reptiles, turtles); Lepidosauria (lizards, snakes, rhynchocephalians, mosasaurs, and others); Archosauria ("ruling reptiles": crocodiles; thecodonts; the two groups of dinosaurs, saurischians and ornithischians; pterosaurs); Ichthyopterygia (extinct aquatic reptiles, the ichthyosaurs); Euryapsida (extinct reptiles, notably the aquatic nothosaurs and plesiosaurs); and Synapsida (the mammal-like reptiles that gave rise to mammals). Reptiles are ectothermic and are characterized by the amniotic egg that can be laid on land. Reptiles were the dominant terrestrial vertebrates during the Mesozoic Era, and the first occur as fossils in late Carboniferous deposits.

**Rudist:** A group of bivalve molluscs that lived only in the Cretaceous Period. They superficially resembled corals and were reef dwellers.

**Saurischian:** The group (Order Saurischia) of reptile-hipped dinosaurs, all of which have a three-pronged pelvis. Saurischians include the theropods and sauropodomorphs.

**Sauropod:** A group (Infraorder Sauropoda) of saurischian (reptile-hipped) dinosaurs that lived from the mid-Jurassic to the late Cretaceous. Sauropods were long, gigantic, quadrupedal herbivores, of which *Diplodocus* and *Apatosaurus* are among the best known.

**Sauropodomorph:** One of the two major groups (Suborder Sauropodomorpha) of saurischian (reptile-hipped) dinosaurs. They were semi-bipedal, or fully quadrupedal and herbivorous. The two subgroups of sauropodomorphs are the infraorders Prosauropoda and Sauropoda.

**Solnhofen:** A series of quarries in the lithographic limestone in Bavaria of late Jurassic age, noted for the excellent preservation of many invertebrates, fish, rhynchosaurs, pterosaurs, dinosaurs, and especially, the earliest known bird, *Archaeopteryx*.

**Stegosaur:** A group (Suborder Stegosauria) of ornithischian (bird-hipped) dinosaurs commonly known as the plated dinosaurs because of the series of plates and spines arranged in a double alternating row along the entire length of the vertebral column. Stegosaurs were herbivorous, quadrupedal, and have been recovered only from late Jurassic and early Cretaceous deposits.

**Synapsid:** A group of reptiles that gave rise to mammals at the end of the Triassic Period. Synapsids were the dominant land reptiles during the Permian and Triassic, but were supplanted after the Triassic by the archosaurian reptiles. Some lineages of synapsids (the Therapsids or mammal-like reptiles) evolved hair, upright stance, partial endothermy and other characteristics typical of mammals. Skulls of synapsid reptiles had a single temporal opening (opening in the temporal area on either side of the skull), whereas some other reptiles, such as archosaurs and lepidosaurs, had two temporal openings on each side of the skull.

**Thecodont:** A major group (Order Thecodontia) of archosaurian reptiles from which all other archosaurs, including dinosaurs, evolved. Fossil thecodonts are known from the late Permian to the late Triassic. They were mostly small, partially bipedal or quadrupedal reptiles with a three-pronged pelvis. The term "thecodont" means "teeth implanted in sockets."

**Theropod:** One of the two major groups (Suborder Theropoda) of saurischian (reptile-hipped) dinosaurs. Theropods, known from the mid-Triassic to the late Cretaceous, were bipedal carnivores.

**Triassic:** The first period (before the Jurassic and Cretaceous) of the Mesozoic Era, from approximately 245 to 208 million years ago. Dinosaurs and mammals appeared during the Triassic.

**Tyrannosaur:** A family of large, bipedal, carnivorous saurischian (reptile-hipped) dinosaurs that lived world-wide during the late Cretaceous. *Tyrannosaurus rex* is probably the most famous member of the group.

**Vertebrate:** All animals that possess a vertebral column (backbone). The living groups of vertebrates are: agnathans (jawless fish: the lamprey and hagfish); bony fish; cartilaginous fish (sharks, skates, rays); amphibians; reptiles; birds; and mammals.

# Notes

**1**
This acount of Carnegie's interest in dinosaurs is grounded on an account chronicled in *Carnegie Magazine* and written by Arthur S. Coggeshall, a pioneer in dinosaur work here at Carnegie Museum. See Coggeshall's article and a brief *vita* in "How Dippy Came to Pittsburgh," *Carnegie Magazine*, 25 (September, 1951), 238-240.

**2**
Coggeshall, p. 240.

**3**
Anonymous. Popular as an old college song. Found in Chapter 17 "The Presentation of *Diplodocus*," in *To the River Plate and Back* by W.J. Holland (New York: G.P. Putnam's Sons, 1913).

**4**
Earl Douglass, letter to W.J. Holland (26 August, 1909), in possession of Carnegie Museum of Natural History, Section of Vertebrate Fossils. All subsequent letters included in references are in the possession of the Museum's Section of Vertebrate Fossils.

**5**
Douglass, letter to Holland (28 December, 1909).

**6**
Douglass, letter to Holland (4 November, 1909).

**7**
Holland, letter to Douglass (12 January, 1916).

**8**
Douglass, letter to Dr. Charles D. Walcott (7 March, 1923).

**9**
Douglass, letter to Holland (18 January, 1927).

**10**
F. Krantz, letter to J.B. Hatcher (30 October, 1902), reprint in possession of Museum's Section of Vertebrate Fossils.

**11**
Holland, letter to Andrew Carnegie (9 May, 1903).

**12**
Holland, letter to Carnegie (8 June, 1903), reprint in possession of Museum's Section of Vertebrate Fossils.

**13**
Holland, letter to James Bertram (21 September, 1903).

**14**
Because techniques for processing samples are constantly being refined, there are variations in dates from source to source. To insure consistency in this book, all references to dates of the Mesozoic Era have been taken from Richard Lee Armstrong, "Contributions to the Geologic Time Scale," in *Pre-Cenozoic Phanerozoic Time Scale—Computer File of Critical Dates and Consequences of New and In-Progress Decay-Constant Revisions,* Studies in Geology, No. 6 (Tulsa, OK: American Association of Petroleum Geologists, 1978), pp. 73-91.

# For Further Reading

Charig, Alan. *A New Look at the Dinosaurs.* London: William Heinemann Ltd., 1979.

Colbert, Edwin. *Men and Dinosaurs.* New York: Dutton, 1968.

Desmond, Adrian J. *The Hot-Blooded Dinosaurs.* New York: Dial Press, 1976.

Halstead, L.B. *Dinosaurs.* New York: Sterling Publishing Company, 1981.

Kurtén, Björn. *The Age of the Dinosaurs.* New York: McGraw-Hill, 1968.

Lambert, David. *Dinosaurs.* New York: Crown Publishers, Inc., 1978.

Ostrom, John H. "A New Look at Dinosaurs." *National Geographic,* 154 (August 1978), 152-185.

Russell, Dale. *A Vanished World: The Dinosaurs of Western Canada.* Chicago: University of Chicago Press, 1977.

Steel, Rodney and Anthony Harvey, eds. *The Encyclopedia of Prehistoric Life.* New York: McGraw-Hill, 1979.

White, Theodore. *Dinosaurs at Home.* New York: Vantage Press, 1967.

Wood, Peter, et al. *Life Before Man.* The Emergence of Man Series. New York: Time-Life Books, 1972.

# Index

Author Helen J. McGinnis became enamored with the massive dinosaur collection of Carnegie Museum of Natural History, Carnegie Institute, when she joined the Museum's Section of Vertebrate Fossils as a Research Assistant in 1970. This interest and the long-felt need for a popular guide to the Hall and a written history of the collection led her to undertake the ambitious task of researching and writing the present volume.

Ms. McGinnis received a B.A. in Zoology and an M.A. in Paleontology from the University of California at Berkeley. She also holds a Master of Science degree in Wildlife Management from the Pennsylvania State University. In addition to her work at Carnegie Museum of Natural History, Carnegie Institute, Ms. McGinnis has held positions at the Smithsonian Institution and at the Museum of Vertebrate Zoology and the Museum of Paleontology at the University of California, Berkeley. Currently residing in Mississippi, her writing now deals primarily with environmental problems and wildlife.